Table of C

Introduction   7

Chapter 1 :   The Road Back to You   11
               Carole Blackburn

Chapter 2:   Moving Forward With Failure   21
               Caron Bernard

Chapter 3:   From Rags to Riches   31
               Louisa Tam

Chapter 4:   A Conversation with the Moon   41
               Lesa Ritchie Craig

Chapter 5:   Let Light Guide You Home   49
               Crystal MacGregor

Chapter 6:   From Pain to Purpose   59
               Lesley James

Chapter 7:   Prioritize Protecting Yourself   69
               Sara Curleigh-Parsons

Chapter 8:   You Do Matter!   79
               Janet H. Lau

Chapter 9:   Take Flight   89
               Ada S. Lau

Chapter 10:   Nature's Path to Confidence   99
              Karen S. Richter

Chapter 11:   A Second Chance at Life   109
              Antonietta Botticelli

Chapter 12:   Finding the Strength   117
              Amy P. K. Wong

Chapter 13:   A Soul Makeover Journey   125
              Sandra Didomenico

Chapter 14:   Untethered from the 'Should'   135
              Nicole Woodcox Bolden

Chapter 15:   Everyone Has a Story   145
              Christa Greenland

Chapter 16:   The Lifeline I Didn't Know I Needed   153
              Julie Clark Wobbe

Chapter 17:   Listening to Your Inner Voice   163
              Carol Ward

Chapter 18:   The Gift of Giving   173
              Marcia Agius

Chapter 19:   We Are the Light We Seek in the World   183
              Shruti Singh

Chapter 20:   Feed Your Soul   191
               Tammy Hudgin

Chapter 21:   Becoming the Light   201
               Lisa Pinnock

Acknowledgments   211

Introduction

"We are called to be a light for others. This much I know to be true. But first, we must find our own radiance and let it shine from within."
-Unknown

As I contemplate these words and how they've shaped my recent journey, I'm awe-struck by the number of factors that have come together to make this book a reality. The word "serendipity" comes to mind. And when these kinds of happy accidents occur several times over, you tend to sit up and take notice.

We've likely all experienced moments like this one, when things happen seemingly by chance or coincidence. On deeper reflection, there's nothing accidental about them. These occurrences are by design and invite us to pause and soak in the wonders of life. You've heard the saying, "When the student is ready, the teacher appears." Well, I didn't realize it, but I was about to get schooled!

Rewind to the Fall of 2020 . . . my first co-authored book, *Women, Let's Rise*, had recently launched, and what a whirlwind of excitement that entailed! I'm forever grateful for the opportunity to be a spoke in that wheel. Thanks to my dear friend Lola Tsai Small who introduced me to the project. The entire writing journey was a trial by fire in the best ways possible. I learned to listen within for guidance, trust the process before knowing the "how-to's," and tap into an inner strength I had previously underestimated. All skills and outlooks that would serve me well in the months to come.

Another key learning moment for me was the experience of writing as a form of healing—one in which we can find strength in vulnerability. I had finally discovered an outlet that not only worked for self-expression, but was also a gateway to a deeper level of self-awareness and empowerment. And I was hooked!

Now here's where things get interesting: a little seed had been planted during my first authorship project, and I wondered if maybe I could initiate a similar experience for women, with a concept that I would develop and nurture to fruition. I can't say that it was a burning desire that I set out to pursue with great determination. At least, not at the outset. Rather, it was a gentle ebb and flow of ideas, visualizations, and, eventually, clear-as-day downloads from God/ Spirit/Universal Source. And it centered every single concept that surfaced on the light or source energy that comes from within. But how do we shine our lights brightly when we've lost touch with who we are? It was this point of inquiry that resonated deeply and kept calling me back for further reflection. And that's how *Uncover Your Light: Empowering Stories of Hope and Resilience* was born.

"If you build it, they will come," the famously misquoted line from the 1989 movie *Field of Dreams* is so appropriate to describe what happened next. It's one thing to feel in your bones that your idea is worthwhile, but it's another thing altogether to put it to the test with real, live people . . . other than your mom! Fast forward to March 2021 and, after getting the green light from our publisher, I set out to find twenty willing souls to join me on this writing adventure. Yeah, no pressure! But here's what I found: The more I spoke about uncovering my light, the more, "Aha's," and "Me too's," I heard from the diverse group of women I encountered. Not to mention the connections that would literally fall into my lap, as if a magnetic force was moving this project on waves of forward momentum. This happened so frequently that a second volume of *Uncover Your Light* was conceived in June of 2021 and will be published in August 2022!

I share this progression of events, not to pat myself on the back—although we, as women, need to do more of that, unapologetically—but to affirm what I regard as truth in recent years: When we say a brave "yes" to opportunity, the Universe has our backs and things will unfold in a myriad of unexpected ways. It's pretty remarkable, just wait and see!

My deep gratitude goes out to the talented, heart-centered, courageous women I had the honor of working alongside to create our compilation, *Uncover Your Light*. These stories of hope and strength are about being the best version of yourself, which is a profound act of self-love. The twenty co-authors who share their stories have faced their fears when the path ahead seemed dark and unknown, and they want to provide a roadmap for others who are on similar journeys. They offer insights from lived experiences that can serve as a survival guide for women from all walks of life.

Our co-authors live in three different countries—Canada, the U.S., and England—but they represent a greater spectrum of diversity than their geographical locations would show. The array of various backgrounds and cultures has created a rich tapestry of experiences that come through in their writings. Their professions cover a wide range—from life coaching, health and wellness, finance, education, philanthropy, entrepreneurship, and more.

The topics within these chapters are widely relatable, yet deeply personal and unique. They address issues such as family breakdown and rebuilding life from scratch, personal trauma and upheaval, journeys of self-discovery and finding your inner strength, discovering your worth and living with purpose, and so much more. You, our dear reader, will walk away with fresh insights, life lessons, and a multitude of practical tips that you can implement in your daily life.

What does it mean to uncover *your* light? How would that unfold in *your* personal situation?

What would the process look and *feel* like? For each of us, the answers will be vastly different. But the ways in which we approach life's challenges, and the tools we use to overcome them, are intertwined with common threads. Through these words, our intention is to give you a framework to begin to unravel any complexities that may exist in your life. When we shine our lights brightly, we become beacons of hope radiating throughout the world, and we unconsciously give others permission to do the same.

Each of us has a voice and message that matters, and bringing them to light will create ripple effects that will last beyond the lifespan of this book. This is how we can change both our inner landscapes and the outer world—by witnessing our truths, one story at a time.

Many of the courageous women, whose stories unfold in these pages, have experienced life transitions and the mental and emotional trauma that often comes with them. In some cases, they experienced a gradual detachment and wandering from self after putting everyone else first and only taking whatever breadcrumbs were left over. Does any of this sound familiar? In every case, the authors tapped into an inner wellspring of hope and resilience, allowing their unique beings to be unearthed and illuminated.

I'm so proud of what each co-author has brought to this project, because these words reflect their authentic selves, no holds barred or window dressing needed. And I'm super excited for you, our valued reader, to delve into these chapters and see which parts resonate the most. I invite you to activate all of your senses as you read, imagining yourself on the journey beside each woman. You may be surprised by the number of times you find yourself nodding your head in agreement, or yelling out, "Heck yeah!" in solidarity. We welcome these affirmations because they're signs of a knowing sisterhood and shared understanding.

As I read through these poignant stories over the months of our writing project, I was reminded of something I wrote years ago in *Women Let's Rise*. Talk about foreshadowing!

"In this life, we get to own what we know to be true. We need to struggle at times and face adversity head-on in order to build resilience, but we don't have to face these moments alone: we can turn to others for support and guidance."

We are humbled and honored that you have chosen to turn to this book for a dose of support and guidance. Our sincere wish is that you'll find an abundance of inspiration for the journey.

Introduction by Lisa Pinnock

Chapter 1
The Road Back to You

Carole Blackburn

"The more I pay attention to what makes me feel less than worthy or less than valued in any area of my life, the more I can see what I need to do to never feel that way again. Embrace the change that challenges you to grow."

Carole Blackburn is a Certified Coach and Motivational Speaker who specializes in empowering women to reclaim their life's passion and purpose. Through transformational coaching practices, Carole has helped many women break free from feeling stuck and unfulfilled in their lives. Her passion is to continue to reach women who need the support, motivation, and accountability to step into their greatness.

Over the past five years, Carole has delivered her message of awakening women to their unlimited and untapped potential on stages and within businesses and organizations. With over twelve years of experience in personal and professional growth, her focus has been on empowering women to build their confidence and to break through their glass ceilings.

Carole knows first hand what it takes to thrive amidst challenging experiences. Her personal transformation from adversity to triumph has been incredible and has enabled a lifestyle of deep meaning and purpose. Carole lives in Ottawa, Ontario, Canada with her two children.

www.caroleblackburn-lifecoach.com

ig: caroleblackburn.lifecoach ~ fb: Carole.BlackburnLifeCoach

li: Carole Blackburn ~ t: CaroleCoach1

S trength, resiliency, overcoming, awakening. These four pillars bolstered me after a period of deep self-discovery. Finally, after the most challenging and life-changing two years, my life stands on a solid foundation of love, faith, trust, and intuition.

But this renewal did not come without a cost.

I often refer to the darkest time in my personal journey as the death of my old self and the rebirth of the person I was.

It was late 2008 when things really started to surface from within. My kids were very young at the time—a toddler and a baby. One late afternoon, as they were happily playing together, surrounded by their favorite toys, I was making dinner in the kitchen and talking to my husband on the phone. He informed me he would be late again and not to expect him for dinner. After I hung up, overwhelmed with disappointment, I felt so much loneliness and a deep sense of pain. Sheer exhaustion weighed me down, and I could hear a voice in my head asking, "How did I end up here? This wasn't the way it was supposed to be."

I stood in that kitchen, looking at my happy children, and immediately felt so much guilt and shame for questioning my life.

How could I be so ungrateful? I had the freedom to be at home with my children full-time and live a life that was picture perfect. How dare I question whether I could be more and do more when I had a life that appeared to be flawless? Who was I to speak up and voice my hopes and my goals, when my role was to be the supporter, nurturer, and the one who kept our little family together?

Growing up, I had a sense of who I wanted to be. Someone who would be a leader, a change-maker, or, "A boss of something," as my mom would say. I would imagine myself on the cover of CEO Magazine, confidently sporting a power suit like the kind that prominent women leaders wore. I wanted that sense of accomplishment, but also to make a mark in the world. I wanted to make a difference. I guess you could say I was a young feminist, even though at that time, feminism was portrayed as radical and, sadly, so misinterpreted.

As the youngest child of four and the only girl, I definitely had to make my mark in my family. I was often called "feisty" and "bubbly" maybe because I had a carefree quality that shone through. Or maybe it was because I demanded attention, ranking last in our family birth order. Whatever it was, I knew when I wanted something and I went after it. I was a determined kid.

I drew so much of my strength and independence from my mother. She was a hardworking woman who prioritized her family first, even if it meant sacrificing herself. My mother immigrated to Canada from Lebanon in the 1950s when she was seventeen years old. Prior to leaving Lebanon, after her own mother had died, she had been required to take full responsibility for her four siblings and her father.

Like me, she too had a burning desire to make her own way in the world. But sadly, she never had the opportunity to see it through; her life had to conform to what was expected of her.

I tell you this because my roots formed by watching the hard work and dedication that my mother gave to my family. I witnessed a strong woman put her dreams on hold to raise her family so that we could be successful and have a better life. Doing something— anything—for herself was never an option.

Like most children, I became more and more exposed to the real world as I grew up. Through the school system, religious beliefs, social norms, and media, girls are taught that it is our responsibility to keep our homes in order, raise our children, and support our husband's dreams because that was a woman's place.

I now see how expectations took shape and inform how my life was "supposed" to unfold. These limiting definitions of womanhood were modeled by society, by the biggest influences in my life, and, I have to say, by my mother, however unintentionally. She came from a life of scarcity and even harsher expectations than I ever faced.

Hindsight reveals the path taken versus the one that was divinely created for us. I believe my path took a turn in my early twenties. I remember, time and time again, feeling an enormous pressure to keep up with my best friends and other young women around me, who all seemed to have it figured out. Get a college or university degree, land a job, get married, buy a house, and have kids. This was what I should be pursuing, I suppose. For some reason, I felt I was behind. I felt like they were all sailing away and I stood on the shore, desperate to have what they had.

But how could I have what everyone else had if I wanted completely different things? I wanted to go into the workforce once I finished College and build my career. The thought of traveling and having new experiences excited me, and was something that I wanted to do while I was young. Marriage and family were always a hope, but at that time they were far from my radar in my early twenties. I felt like I either had to follow the flow of the world around me, or take a path that I had to charter on my own.

Little by little, and over a long period, I questioned my inner guide. The trust I'd had in myself as a young, carefree child was fading. The inner confidence and wisdom that I had relied on for all these years, modeled by a strong woman like my mother, became overpowered by the voices of the world around me.

I had to fit into what society was doing (at least that is what I thought back then): Find the husband, buy the house, have the kids, and embark on what was sought after. So, there I was, in my kitchen at thirty-five years old, I had what society told me I should want. Yet, I was gradually giving up pieces of who I was and questioning my life, wondering who I was and where I lost sight of my passions and purpose. I remember asking God to show me where I was supposed to be.

Little did I know, over the next two years everything that made us look like a perfect little family would crumble. The house of cards came crashing down. In those two years, the cracks in my marriage became too difficult to hide. We separated and divorced quickly. During that time, I suffered from feeling like a complete failure, feeling like everything that was supposed to work out had crashed and burned, feeling abandoned and alone. It stripped away much of my inner power, leaving me exposed, like I was under a microscope.

When I asked for revelation and transparency, the universe responded, despite my best efforts of praying for the cracks of my life to be neatly mended. Life was hard and turbulent all the time. Everything was changing quickly. I was navigating stormy waters and desperately trying to survive. The logistical aspects of dismantling a marriage were one thing, the internal self-criticism was another.

"How could I let this happen?"

"Maybe if I had changed, I could have fixed everything?"

"Where did I go wrong?"

I couldn't see past the hurt and pain, and I assumed all the responsibilities of how my marriage had broken down. There was so much that I blamed myself for. Not being a good enough wife and mother. Not feeling like I was worth fighting for. The storm raged inside of me, tearing apart everything that I thought I knew about who I was and what I wanted.

Looking back, I see I needed to face the storm in order to see the clearing.

The aftermath of that part of my life breaking down was literally what I needed to open my eyes to a world of endless possibilities.

November 2010 was the beginning of my self-discovery journey and the road back to me.

The kids and I started over. Not one thing was transferred from the old life to this new one. We started from scratch, like a blank canvas. This is never an easy feat. I stood at a fork in the road and I had a choice: Either I could let this life tear me down, or I could trust my wisdom and the truth of who I was and live unapologetically and authentically as the person I was.

With the moral support of family and friends, my children and I began a new journey together. I made a commitment to myself to focus on healing and growing. That is when I immersed myself in personal growth and self-improvement.

I brought myself into the mix of my life. I nurtured myself and truly saw how I could love myself, even after a dark period of self-loathing.

As each day passed, I gained more and more confidence in knowing that I can be an amazing woman, mother, and live a fulfilled life by design. I could have it all! But it took effort and drive. It took everything in me to gain the momentum that I needed to bring me to where I am today.

I needed to let go of the fear of getting to know who I was all over again. Loneliness is crippling, and it's easy to find something—anything—to distract you from it. But the deepest lessons came when I sat with myself and really tried to get to the woman who was waiting deep inside. Through the pain and the failures, acceptance, healing, and rebirth were waiting on the other side, and were all I needed to see who I really was.

I refused to take on the victim mentality that many would try to put on me by labeling me as the "poor single mom." I am way too stubborn to let that happen, so I decided this is where I needed to show up fully for myself to be an exceptional mother and role model to these two precious children watching me and taking it all in.

Do you know any women who experience that sense of feeling lost in their life? Of not knowing who they are anymore? The more open I am and the more I share my story, the more women say to me, "Yes, me too!"

As we go through our lives, our hopes and dreams are slowly placed on a shelf and we focus instead on attaining the kinds of lives we were taught to value. We are expected to sacrifice our desires and needs to cater to the needs of the world around us. We often silence our voices, not saying what we desperately want in life, for fear of sounding demanding or aggressive.

There is this unspoken rule that many women obey. We smile and project how "happy" we are, even though we suffer in silence and things feel like a mess deep down inside. Too afraid to speak up or too afraid to change our minds, we internalize the fear of appearing to be selfish or unappreciative of what we already have.

For generations, women have been told what their roles should be. There is this sense of obligation to conform to the "rules" of society. We are told to pursue what is revered as the "dream life," instead of carving our own path.

I knew many years ago that I was compromising a great deal in order to feel like I could fit in. And with each step, I was walking a path that was taking me away from who I was. It was gradual and unintentional. And that light within me, guiding me on my journey, grew dimmer and dimmer.

But like any road, there is always a way back to where you belong if you allow your heart and intuition to guide you.

That road took me out of weeds and into a place where I have never felt so free and full of joy!

Now, as I raise my teenage kids, I thank God each day for giving me the strength to let go of the past and build a life I am in love with, one that has offered me the courage to stretch myself past my limitations, a life where taking care of myself is a priority, and where that self-love overflows into motherhood, my business, the women I have the pleasure of walking alongside in their journey, and every single aspect of my world. A life that I am living on my own terms without the pressures of what is expected of me.

It's never too late to answer the call within. It doesn't need to take a personal crisis to wake up. All we need to do is listen to the still voice that has always been there, but has been silenced for so long.

As time goes on and the expectations become louder, the world's voices can overpower your own voice, just as they did my own. But that only leads you off your own path.

However, you too can feel like your life is built on a solid foundation of your deepest values. Your glow will overflow into each part of your life and the love you have for yourself will be felt by those around you.

We speak of changing the world for future generations, and I strongly believe that entails changing the world for our generation so our daughters and granddaughters can learn by example how to believe in themselves and pursue their desires in life. We must come back to who we are and be in touch with what we want out of life. We all have unique attributes to cultivate and share, and doing so makes our lives and the world around us better.

If we don't model how to put our own needs first, the consequence for future generations is that they too will question who they are and what their purpose is and they will have no guidance on how to find themselves. They will lose themselves without knowing where it began.

So, here is what I want to leave you with . . .

Can you learn to trust yourself and be open to saying *yes* to the inner confidence and inner voice that has guided you all along? Can you do this even when you feel overwhelmed and when self-doubt is crippling you? Are you able to allow curiosity to help you explore, without expectations, what possibilities are waiting for you, even if you don't know where to start?

The more you can learn to trust yourself and to see all the unique gifts you have, the brighter your light will shine. The inner voice that guided you all along will lead you to the road you are meant to travel.

And the time is now. Time for change begins today, and it begins with you. It does not wait to begin when it is convenient for everyone else, not when you reach the next milestone in life, not when you finish that to-do list that seems to never end. Today, just as you are, I invite you to reclaim your power, allow your beautiful life to blossom, and find the woman who stands strong inside of you.

Chapter 2
Moving Forward With Failure

Caron Bernard

"What we often view as failure is actually the experience of moving closer to where our heart knows we need to be, and sometimes it takes time for our minds to catch up."

Caron lives in London with her husband and three children and has always been passionate about helping and empowering others.

After stepping away from a career as a barrister, her life changed considerably. It didn't turn out quite how she expected—she tried many roles and projects to get her life "back on track," from starting a healthy food business to doing charity work. Caron's quest to build a better life for herself and her family has given her resilience, compassion, and self-love.

With over twelve years of coaching experience in schools in and around London, Caron has coached hundreds of teenagers in self-awareness, building their confidence, and helping to foster in them a sense of self-belief, whilst at the same time nurturing her own.

Caron now runs an organization that empowers young women of color to succeed in education and their future careers. The organization engenders the belief that through lending a helping hand and building each other up, it can provide a network of women supporting the next generation of women, so they can thrive in years to come.

www.kinshipbursary.co.uk

ig: caronb301 ~ fb: Caron Bernard

li: Caron Bernard ~ Goodreads: Caron

There wasn't one life-defining event that led me to where I am today—leading an organization that supports the progress of young women of color through education and beyond. After a series of failures, I now wake each morning with passion and purpose. I have the privilege of encouraging, empowering, and seeing young minds open to their true power and potential to learn, grow, and effect change. I get to learn of their challenges, their deepest fears, and their successes, and sometimes, in the quiet, I get to watch them blossom and bloom into truly remarkable young women.

Through my dysfunctional childhood, I learned to live in fear. However, I eventually taught myself to read the signs that led me to the life I now enjoy. It was by no means a simple road, but every failure (and there were many) brought me closer to where my heart knew I needed to be.

I was born and grew up in South London, the youngest of four children. My parents arrived in England from Jamaica in the early 1960s as part of the Windrush generation, recruited by the British government following World War II to address a shortage of workers in transport, hospitals, and the postal service. Like many of that generation, Dad grew up in an environment where corporal punishment was normal, so he taught us what he knew—mistakes were punishable by beating, chores had to be done properly, and no one—except for him—was beyond reproach. He worked at London Transport as a bus conductor, spent his spare time meeting up with family and friends, down at the pub, or at the bookies. He had a terrible temper; and was fearsome; he was renowned and revered for it. Mum came from a middle-class family in Kingston, born the third of four girls. She had an adventurous spirit and followed her best friend to England to become a nurse. This sense of adventure would continue throughout our childhood, with summers spent exploring coastal towns up and down the country.

At home, Mum was understated, gentle, kind, and generous. She lived a humble life, but was fiercely protective of her independence and encouraged us to be the same. She taught me I shouldn't rely on anyone for anything.

Leaders Like Us

Mum's relaxed approach toward most things evolved. Like so many first generation Caribbeans living in England, she left parents, sisters and close family behind in Jamaica. Mum became an adult and a parent without the emotional and financial support of having close family nearby and it is only now, as a parent myself, that I appreciate how difficult that must have been. When I was thirteen years old, Dad died in a road traffic accident and it left Mum to bring four of us up alone. She worked hard to ensure our basic needs were met and was concerned about living day to day rather than about what we aspired to become. When I was sixteen, I knew I wanted to travel the world. I studied travel and tourism at college, and that year spent the summer in Jamaica with my maternal grandparents and aunt. Aunt Sal (Salma) was a barrister; she was fierce and forthright. She put everyone in their place—man, woman, and child. In Jamaica, our close friends and family were all professionals—lawyers, doctors, engineers. The seed was sown and for the first time I contemplated life as a professional: Why couldn't this be me?

I loved the freedom and independence of returning to Jamaica year after year, which I did for the next few years. It meant that every year, I was surrounded by people like me in roles of power and leadership. I did not know then the significance of this lesson, which now forms a fundamental aspect of our KINShiP community. The KINShiP Bursary mentoring program recruits women in industry and leadership, who give freely of their time to help inspire the next generation, and our girls get to network and interact with leaders representative of the diverse communities in which they live.

I studied law and pursued a career as a barrister. I see now what I did not recognize at the time: After experiencing a childhood where conflict was normalized, I had come to detest confrontation, which was a crucial element of legal advocacy. Passionate about helping others less able to represent themselves, I secured a scholarship and eventually gained a Master's degree in International Human Rights Law, and successfully completed the Bar.

Accepting the Things You Cannot Change

Shortly after qualifying at the Bar, I got married in Jamaica, my spiritual home. On our return to England, we discovered we were pregnant with identical twins. I cried inconsolably—our lives were about to change, and we weren't prepared for just how much. I would go on to resent this change for a long time. Losing control over the decisions I *wanted* to make because of the decisions I *had* to make caused me great anguish. Growing up, my family had taught me that if I didn't like something, regardless of whether it was in my control, I should change it. Finding out I was having twins flew in the face of this childhood rationale.

I recall watching my grandmother pace up and down in anger if anyone did anything she thought was wrong or unreasonable. She spent time mumbling and pacing and pacing and mumbling. Mum replicated this. I too would try to change situations and people if I didn't like them. So, my early years of marriage were difficult, but slowly (and I mean slowly) I accepted our stark differences. I was driven, ambitious, and unforgiving of myself, and my husband was the complete opposite. I resented being knocked off course by having twins. After all, pursuing a legal career is not as straightforward with two energetic, anarchic, and discombobulating twin boys in tow. My reluctance to accept my reality unwittingly made my life more painful. I tried different jobs and attempted to start businesses I thought were a good fit for my new lifestyle, but I always felt like a failure. I yearned to be practicing law like my friends I went to university with.

Many years later, a close friend confided she thought the boys were the best things that happened to me. They made me more resilient, compassionate, and accepting of others. Through reading self-help books and being more receptive to prayer, meditation, and mindfulness, I learned to be open to me not needing to have a stranglehold on everything in my life, and that there was real power in surrendering to your circumstances.

Back on Track

As the boys grew, I filled their lives with activity after activity, exposing them to every sport and academic endeavor imaginable so that we could find what they excelled in. I gained a sense of purpose, knowing I was doing my best for them. When the boys were toddlers, I tried to see if I could return to the legal field in some capacity. I worked as a trainer for a legal publishing firm, but resented my time away from the boys, and also continued to feel like a failure every moment I was not practicing law. I continued to dream up ways I could go into teaching or lecturing in law but none of these options seemed feasible at the time.

One day, while at the boys' swimming lessons, I met a lovely, soulful, goddess woman named Kuumba. Kuumba was inherently nurturing, bringing love, harmony, and balance to everyone she encountered. Over the coming weeks, we made a habit of chatting and laughing in the thirty-minute spurts of swimming lesson time. In one of our chats, Kuumba mentioned she thought I would make a good life coach.

But I'm a lawyer, I thought to myself. This was the start of my journey into self-development and discovery. I trained as a coach to help students aged fourteen to sixteen with their confidence and self-esteem. I coached part time while continuing to work in the city. I loved it, and slowly I was returning to my true self.

When I was younger, I studied sociology in high school. Different peoples and societies fascinated me. I rekindled this passion in my work as a coach. The many heartfelt and revealing moments the students shared, the stories of their vulnerability and sincerity, it all felt like a mirror exposing my sensitivities, which I could not express at their age. The experience of connecting with them helped awaken in me a deeper connection to a side of myself that was long forgotten. I was a sociologist, and the feeling of elation I had when coaching, compared with the dread I felt when I was training for the bar, taught me to appreciate that how I felt was key to knowing who I was.

Run Your Own Race

After five years of trudging in and out on the daily commute, Mum fell ill with cancer. I retired from the city humdrum and spent the following months looking after her. Mum recovered, and I decided I would work part time to ensure I was around for her and my two-year-old daughter. Looking for part time work entailed understating my expertise on my resume, and I ended up taking several dead-end jobs just to stay local.

While studying for the bar, I spent so much time proving to myself what I could become, I forgot to stop and understand who I really was. I was so caught up in building the life of somebody else's dreams I failed to pay attention to my own yearnings.

My ambitious spirit prevailed. I had always toyed with the idea of starting a business. So, I started my own coaching consultancy. It took months to set up my website, and I was bad at marketing myself, so, regrettably, the business failed. Again, my restless spirit triumphed. I never stopped thinking about the next project and how I could make things better for the world, myself, others . . .

Because of a few motorcycle accidents, my husband kept ending up in the hospital. I brought him healthy food and smoothies, and other patients on the ward suggested making a business of it. Great idea! Another project I could run with: I could sell healthy foods in hospital foyers. I needed experience, so I started out in local food markets. This took a gargantuan effort and the support of friends and family, and before long, I knew it did not suit me. My failures were stacking up, but I was learning so much about myself and about starting a business in the process.

The problem, I see now, was that I kept taking suggestions from others and putting that at the center of my life. I wasn't tuning in to my frequency or listening to my spirit.

In recent years, there has been more information available about being in touch with our bodies or our feelings, but growing up, I was not exposed to these ideas. I was encouraged to power through, regardless of our emotions. Now, I encourage others to ask themselves, "How do I feel in the morning before going to work, or on a Sunday evening before the start of the working week?" If you are filled with anxiety, or days in a row, you wake up feeling lethargic and unfulfilled, then perhaps it's time for a change. Give yourself a time limit and start creating your plan for change.

Getting Closer

As luck would have it, a friend of mine was working with a charity, and they were looking for a tutor. She remembered I had done some tutoring in the past, so invited me to apply. This local charity was doing great things with those most in need in the community, running adult education programs to upskill and support individuals heading back to work. They also ran a team dedicated to children, young people, and families, and I started tutoring at their after-school clubs, helping children with their education. I loved my work, taking part in community-based activities, and helping to support a community characterized by a low socioeconomic status. They soon promoted me to team coordinator and then team manager.

While at the charity, I watched the 2017 BBC documentary, *Will Britain Ever Have a Black Prime Minister?* The program investigated the degree of inequality faced by black people in the UK and highlighted that forty-five percent of black people in the UK lived in poverty. It showed that a person's race is a significant factor explaining underachievement in education and leadership in Britain. The COVID-19 pandemic has amplified the difference, where unemployment rates among young black graduates are significantly higher compared to their white counterparts. The statistics are staggering. I knew that discrimination and unconscious bias were present in the UK, however, I was ignorant of how severe the problem was. I made it my mission to tell everyone I met about these statistics.

I continued my work, coaching and tutoring young people in the community, but these ominous statistics remained in the background. Over a couple of summers, my sons volunteered for the charity; I wanted to ensure that they appreciated the value of giving back and helping others. Though I loved my job, there had been several gang-related incidents in the area, and I knew that the charity needed to widen its focus. I didn't realize it, but I was uncomfortable dealing with a few aspects of my role. I wasn't sure if it was self-sabotage, or my heart leading me to where it knew I needed to be, but they dismissed me from the charity for not enforcing policy. Even though this meant an end to the long hours and the stress of being target-driven and funding-led, I was heartbroken.

However, the termination of my role was a relief in some ways. But now I needed to figure out where to go next. It was time to tune into my frequency. In the quiet, I sat with a blank page before me and listed my values, my skills, and organizations I admired and would want to work for or with. I had come across an organization in the UK providing bursaries for young black men to go to university. This was a great idea, and with everything I'd learned in life so far, I knew I could offer something similar to young women of color. The idea of the KINShiP Bursary was born!

While working on my idea, I needed to find employment, so I began temping as a receptionist for a school for fourteen- to eighteen-year-olds in Brixton. School was the perfect place for me—a place where staff gets to support and inspire young minds. But KINShiP remained secure in my mind. While working at the school, I met Sam, a math teacher who was positive, kind, and funny, and we found we shared so many coincidences. We were reading the same book, our daughters shared a birthday, and Sam shared a birthday with two close friends of mine, and that was just the beginning. Sam and I were on the same page for many things. I told her about KINShiP and that I was looking for a co-director and Sam agreed to come on board. We started KINShiP in the middle of the pandemic with an online coaching provision, online mentoring, and bursary interviews. We are now in three schools and impacting over 200 girls of color this year alone. Our KINShiP journey so far has been smooth-running; the people, facilities, and opportunities have simply presented themselves at the right time.

We are steadily building a network of women supporting the next generation of women so that they can learn to thrive in years to come. We hope to affect social mobility and increase diversity in higher education and leadership, which will be tremendous. Without realizing it, every failure has brought me closer to where my heart knew I needed to be . . . it just took a little time for my brain to catch up.

Chapter 3
From Rags to Riches

Louisa Tam

"The world around you reflects the world within you."

Louisa Tam is a Toronto-based financial advisor. She is one of the most resilient and inspiring people you could meet and spend time with. *Uncover Your Light* is her authorial debut and, through her chapter, she candidly takes us into her chaotic past and how it leads her to connect to her true self.

Over the past decade, Louisa has been working to foster healing and personal growth. Through this, she found the courage to face her old demons and to let them go.

She is not proud of some of her past choices. On this journey within, Louisa learned the past is not a life sentence, and by embracing it, it becomes your strength. She found the power within to rewrite her destiny and continues to grow each day. She hopes her story will find its way into the hearts of women, to shine a light of guidance and optimism in their lives, and to help them through whatever challenge they may be facing.

When Louisa isn't working in her business, she enjoys devoting time to her personal growth, her kids, her family, her life partner, Bruce; teaching spin classes, and playing with their two cats, Emma and Charming.

fb: louisa.tam888 ~ li: Louisa Tam

Growing up as the oldest of three sisters and a brother in a traditional Chinese family was difficult. Many readers from the same culture can probably relate to this. The parental rules were incredibly strict, children didn't speak or have opinions, and no physical affection was given. They gave me clear guidelines regarding who I could be friends with. We went to Chinese School on Saturdays, Buddhist Temple on Sundays, and anything school related came before friends, TV, talking on the phone, or hobbies. Being fashionable and wearing the latest clothing trend was not allowed, neither was makeup nor jewelry. These were unnecessary distractions from school.

As a shy and awkward girl, it felt like a nightmare being at school and I often cried because of the bullying. Faking sickness and complaining about not feeling well were common tactics to escape school, especially if there was a class presentation. I identified with being an outsider, and in high school, I found solace with groups that were out of the limelight.

I wish I could have told the young girl that was me, she had a voice, and she was worthy; to let her know that it's okay to be who you are, to ask for what you want, and to have standards. The affective poverty I was left with because of my limiting beliefs and emotional imbalance smothered my self-confidence in much of my life.

My parents realized that I was conflicted in my teen years and sent me to counseling to talk about my anger. I resented my parents for thinking this was a good idea. The counseling didn't work, since I was completely uninterested and uncooperative. Looking back, my anger and bitter attitude were derived from the lack of freedom to express myself, and the closeness I needed from my parents, especially my mother. I envied my friends who seemed to have a close relationship with their parents. My love for my parents is dear, and I know they did everything to the best of their power and knowledge to love me. The lessons they taught me and the sacrifices they made were invaluable, but I was so closed off that it was impossible for them to communicate with me.

Throughout school, my grades ranged from the forties to sixties. I habitually cut classes and forged notes to get out of things. This eventually led me to drop out of high school.

Fast forward five years: At twenty-one years old, my first son was born. Newly unemployed, living with my son's father, and broke. Fortunately, social assistance for low-income parents helped us with rent and food, but we still needed to scrape our pennies together daily. We lived on Mac n' Cheese, Hamburger Helper, and canned tuna so that we could afford formula, and everything else our son needed. I continuously circled job postings and ads in the newspapers, but finding employment was a challenge. I felt anxious every day, wondering how to support our family and getting our bills paid. After several months of looking, I responded to an ad for lingerie models. Thinking, *How difficult could that be?* My son's dad drove me to my interview, and the next day the job was mine. Progress! I was told to bring an assortment of outfits with me to work. This should have been my first red flag. My judgment was impaired by my happiness in bringing home some income. It was also flattering that someone thought I was attractive enough to be a model. My first day brought about the realization that I was not a model in the sense that I had expected—they asked me to remove clothing as the customer put tips in a jar. This was my first experience with exploitation.

Soon after, I quit but was still desperate for income to keep our home and to feed our family. I went to a club in the east end of the city where we lived for yet another "interview," and they hired me on the spot. This was the beginning of a twelve-year career in an industry that hardened me and nearly damaged my soul for good.

I worked as a dancer in the adult entertainment industry and was very level-headed for the first eight years. I didn't party and maintained high standards for what I would tolerate, which was nothing. Smoking cigarettes was my only vice, a habit that lasted for twenty-plus years. The group of women in my circle shared the same mindset. We kept each other grounded in a very twisted world. It was in this twisted world that I got my first taste of feeling in control. Specifically, I controlled the room, most of the patrons, and I had a lot of money. Making a six-figure income at the age of twenty-two, and saving eighty percent of what I earned daily by investing. My excessive lifestyle, that came easily affordable consisted of: a beautiful home with expensive furniture, eating expensive food, traveling twice a year without having to save up for it, nice cars, expensive clothes, summers off, and I spoiled my family with high-priced gifts. "No" was a word my son never heard from me when he wanted something, and I paid for everything in cash. I felt and lived like a celebrity.

At the age of twenty-nine, all of that had changed. The father of my son and I were no longer together and I found myself in a physically and mentally abusive relationship when I discovered my first chemical drug. While in the change room feeling down about myself and my life, a couple of girls were "dropping" ecstasy. When asked if I could try, they were happy to include me. I took half, and put the other half in my purse. Within half an hour, all of my bad feelings were gone and I was on cloud nine. This led to more drug use, including cocaine, which spawned a lifestyle of after-hours parties, substance abuse, and a lack of respect for myself or my family. I put myself into a ghost state from morning to night. By doing this, I locked my heart in a box and threw away the key—staying numb to avoid facing my demons, my fears, and my truths.

It only took two years to lose everything I had. I was couch surfing, going from one place to another, while all of my belongings were scattered between my parents' house and storage. My life was like this for a couple of years.

My struggle with hard drugs had many facets. It was about not feeling pain, not caring, and most of all, not facing the real me. Drug abuse led me spiraling down on a path of dangerous choices and abusive relationships. A lifeless appearance, and at five foot two, I weighed around a hundred pounds. I went from a shy little girl into an erratic person, always yelling, "Hey everyone, look at me and look how great I am!" I treated my family like garbage and they kept me at arm's length. Most of my life was spent not liking who I was, trying to be someone else, changing my personality to "fit in" with whoever my friends were. I was confined by my fears of not measuring up, not being good enough, pretty enough, interesting enough . . . for years.

At the age of thirty, my doctor put me on antidepressants. Amusingly, my response to her was I didn't want them because I didn't want to become addicted. She looked at me matter-of-factly, and said, "So, you'll take street drugs, but you won't take mine?"

I took her advice and was on those antidepressants for the next two years.

That same year, I became sick and tired of my lifestyle: The endless party nights, lack of sleep, having no self-worth, and coasting aimlessly through life. I walked out of the establishment I was working at and never went back. My road to recovery seemed quite smooth, which is rarely the case. Luckily, I didn't experience physical withdrawals, nor did I think about numbing myself anymore. I embellished my experiences for the past ten years and referred to it as "sales" on my resume and got a job as a retail store manager. I joined a gym, replacing my substance addiction with working out—getting into shape was my new drug.

Life was brighter as I reintegrated myself into a more conventional lifestyle. I was completely immersed in fitness and made friends with people in the industry. I loved learning about workouts and becoming physically fit. I was the healthiest I had ever been, enjoying conversations about workout routines and fitness competitions. My wardrobe went from nightclub-style to fitness-model-style. It was in this world, at the gym where I regularly worked out, that I met the young man who would become my husband.

At age thirty-four I was married, and had my second son the following year. My dream of having a family life, doing family things, and finally feeling like a functional and contributing member of society was happening. Going back to school to become a Personal Support Worker, I found that school was enjoyable when it was my choice. Acing the course with a near-perfect grade gave me confidence that I didn't experience in my youth. With the credits I received from graduating, I also earned my high school diploma.

A retirement home and a long-term care home hired me to work the overnight shift, which I did for several years. My son was only nine months old. After my overnight shifts, I would come home and get showered, then jump into mom mode. Taking opportunities to nap when he napped, until I put him into bed at 7:30 in the evening. I would then lie down on the couch for a nap before waking up at 9 p.m. to get ready for my shift.

This was my routine for several years.

We lived a fairly simple life, but we, as a couple, had a conflicted relationship. We both came with our own emotional baggage, which bled into our daily lives. We faced money problems soon after buying our home, and more struggles came from that. Just before Christmas 2008, our marriage was over. I came home one night after work to an almost empty house, and my child and husband were gone. I hadn't had the mental capacity to care for my son, since I picked up partying again to deal with my unhappiness. My then-husband did what he felt he needed to do by leaving. The only way I knew how to handle the pain of losing my son was to dive back into a lifestyle of partying and drug abuse. It wasn't long before my car was repossessed, my house foreclosed, and I filed for bankruptcy.

One day, I lay on my son's bed after deliberately overdosing to end my life. As my heart started slowing down, I pictured my family finding me. I imagined their response, my parents and siblings. Then reality struck me when I envisioned my funeral. I thought about what my sons would say about me, and I realized there wasn't anything good to say. I cried. What saved me from my almost successful suicide attempt? My sons. It hit me—they deserved to have a mom they could be proud of. That was the catalyst for my change, and I began putting my life back together once more.

In 2011 after a twenty-three-year habit, I smoked my last cigarette and started running. It changed my life. I became a healthier version of myself, and surrounded myself with other like-minded runners who became my good friends. My partner today whom I met through the same running group, is my biggest cheerleader. Life moves in the direction of the associations you keep. When I turned fifty, my soul shifted. I wouldn't call it a mid-life crisis, but I started looking within myself more deeply and analyzed the person I came to be.

Looking in the mirror and being honest with myself was incredibly uncomfortable for me because, like so many others, I was conditioned to be "perfect." My inward reflection opened up a Pandora's Box of buried, painful feelings, and surprising memories. Doing this work has freed me from the shackles of my past. Over the past ten-plus years, I improved my life through positive associations, learning constructive behaviors, replacing poor habits with healthier ones, revitalizing my attitude, and becoming obsessed with reading and learning. My process wasn't perfect, and it often looked like this: Make progress, feel great about myself, fall back into old attitudes and limiting beliefs, feel like I'll never get "there," and try again. My point is this is okay. Just keep going. I slip and fall, but I get back up. It took years to become the person I was, it will take time to undo the parts of me that I want to change. And that is okay.

What I realized during the pandemic of 2020 was that all the efforts I made were helping me to make some much needed changes in how I approached life, but something was still lacking. My fragile ego had shadowed the core of my being for years. What began as inner work to learn how to physically heal myself through meditation became the work of getting to know my soul. This led to a huge emotional transformation. No longer do I seek superficial validation or attention, and my appearance no longer defines me. Intentional practice in creating a deep awareness of my internal dialogue, recognizing the thoughts that don't serve me, and pushing them out of my mind without judgment. I learned to have compassion for myself, and realized that for many years I was half asleep and on auto-pilot. This is an ongoing journey, and although the version of me that exists today is the best that I have known, it excites me to think of where my path can go. My career path allows me to use my experiences, both successes and failures, to help people. The relationships I have with my family, my kids, and my friends are strengthened—a deep love I never allowed myself to know. I'm not suggesting you become a yogi or that meditation is the answer for you, nor am I saying that it is the only way to find healing or your true purpose. I am only sharing how this path helped me to connect to my authentic self.

Love yourself, you are worth it, and above all, you deserve it. You deserve to affect change in the world around you. Your thoughts and intentions, whether or not you say them out loud, impact every fiber of your being. I could have continued avoiding the parts of my life that I was ashamed and embarrassed of, and carried on living life without curiosity, but it has been so freeing to accept and embrace every piece of my past. This has allowed me to uncover light and richness in life. I shared my story with vulnerability and honesty, hoping to inspire you, my dear reader. The power to design the life you seek lies within you.

Chapter 4
A Conversation with the Moon

Lesa Ritchie Craig

"We don't always have to understand the reasons for the pain or the grief, just maybe the experience is necessary."

Lesa Ritchie Craig is a Certified Health and Nutrition Coach with a focus on Autism, PTSD, anxiety, depression, auto-immune, chromosome disorders, and gut balance. She is an aspiring author, passionate homeschool teacher, student of life, nutrition nerd, and lover of science.

Lesa is enthusiastically devoted to her husband and best friend, who inspires her every day to keep showing up on this journey, to radiate her authentic light, and to live her truth. Their commitment to each other and to their family is the foundation of strength and the guiding light that propels them forward. They are the parents of seven badass humans, three sweet grandbabies, and three furbabies, and they are enjoying every chapter of life.

Lesa's favorite place is the space where science and spirituality meet. She is in absolute awe of all the unexpected blessings. She is so very grateful for the lessons—no matter how hard—for they become our story. They shape us. As we give space for others to grow, we honor that we are all connected. We don't have to know all the answers to be whole, to shine. The authentic self knows how to surrender, to trust the process, and to keep showing up in light and love.

vibrantfamilies.com

ig: vibrantfamilies ~ fb: lesaritchiecraig

"Maybe you have to know the darkness before you can appreciate the light."
- Madeline L'Engle

Istood silently in the dark waiting for something, anything, to happen. Frozen. Unable to make my body move. Eventually, I found enough strength to switch on the light and stare at her. I did not recognize the person staring back at me. I forced a breath and the exhale fogged the mirror. I slowly wiped it clean with my towel and leaned in for a closer look. There was something there in her eyes, something I recognized, a glimmer of hope maybe. Long, hot showers had become the norm, the place I could let out the gut-wrenching wails and pray the water would drown out the pain. Is this what grief is supposed to feel like? Nobody had died, nevertheless, this was the worst pain I had ever endured. I felt so alone. Consumed with uncertainty, shame, guilt, anger, and depression. No foreseeable answers, no rituals of closure, just stifling silence.

I felt my entire world crumble beneath me, the tapestry of my life unraveling with one single strand, grasping desperately to hold on, and there was nothing I could do to keep it from unstitching. The fantasy bubble of the future I dreamed about popped in an instant, it left me feeling alone, rejected, and hopeless.

No amount of apologizing or talking made any difference, in fact, it seemed to make everything worse. Everyone's pain was too raw for listening, let alone for acceptance or forgiveness. Nobody was ready to acknowledge the other person's truth or see from the other person's point of view. Everyone says they want an apology, but so often they just want to be right. I was badly wounded, and I could not figure out how to let go of the pain. I wanted to let it go, but the pain held me, not the other way around. How could I loosen the grip that pain had on my heart and my mind? How could I live and breathe again and accept a different future than the one I imagined?

My children and my family are everything to me. I am a planner, my future filled with visions of grandkids running through sprinklers, and my adult children playing games, laughing, having musical jam sessions, and everyone sharing a meal. I am a problem solver, I fix things, but I could not fix this. I am a fighter, I fight for what I love, but I could no longer land a punch. I am an optimist, but I could not see a positive outcome, no matter how hard I tried envisioning the rainbow.

I often daydream of the next family gathering, when we could all be together again. I have adult children who have already left the nest and started careers and families, and I have younger children who depend on me, and teenagers with one foot out the door. It is difficult to balance being present in the moment with the children still at home while longing for the ones who are living life on their own. I am often reminded of my favorite Kahlil Gibran poem, "On Children." It teaches me I am the bow and they are the arrows. I am *not* the Archer. They came through me, but not from me. I must bend in the Archer's hands. I must be strong, stable, and flexible so they can go far. Still, I desire to hold on to them and relive the joy that each one of them has brought into my life. Like a drug, I am addicted to my children. The very thought of my life without them, I lose any sense of rational thinking. The "what ifs" of tomorrow and the regrets of yesterday creep in and wreak havoc on my mind. *What if I never see my children all together again? What if my grandbabies don't know who I am or how much I love them? What if the last family photo is actually the last family photo?* Wishing I could have said all the right words. Regretting that I didn't do something more.

I feel broken, like I had somehow failed. The guilt and shame creep in and compound my emotional injuries. The sense of failure becomes lost in abstract thought, knowing the past won't change, and not wanting to make the same mistakes in the future. The conflict of different emotions battle inside of me, wardens of my mind holding me prisoner. Is the desire to hold on to my children part of my addiction to them, or my need to somehow get "it" right, a do-over? If I did it differently, could I change the outcome? I am the bow, not the Archer. Being "mom" has been my identity for so long that I don't know who I am without them. What is the purpose of the bow when the arrows are gone?

I hoped that the long, hot showers would wash away the pain, but there I was, months later, still with no reprieve. At first, it was just a small glimmer of hope. As I sat alone in the darkness of the room, I felt something gently place a comforting hand on my shoulder. I looked up to see her crescent smile illuminating the corner of my window and casting a shadow against the wall behind me. I'd looked her way a million times, but tonight she was a friend, content in her waxing crescent phase, more than willing to lend a comforting light to guide me. "Do not fear the darkness, it is the necessary part before we can return to the light. It is the time for being still and recharging. It is a time for quieting the mind, turning inward, so we can see what is stuck. It is time to gather what we are holding and release it back into the light. What are you holding on to, my dear?"

I contemplated: "Grief and pain; the wrongs that others have caused me; the guilt of my own actions."

"I see. Then, may I ask, what it is you are seeking?"

I felt at ease, and the answers came more quickly this time, "Clarity. Forgiveness."

Moon's voice was familiar, calm but compelling, "Forgiveness does not come as a result of an apology. If you are seeking an apology in order to forgive, then you are mistaken. Forgiveness is not something we give someone else, it is something we do to release our own selves from pain. Apologizing is not admitting fault. It is acknowledging the other person's pain and hurt and putting the relationship first. An apology can be an offering of empathy and compassion, recognizing that someone else has a different perspective than you, and therefore a different experience. Perhaps trauma is getting in the way, and personal triggers are being processed. Sometimes, an apology is not accepted because personal pain and hurt cloud our clarity, and we simply do not feel heard. Apologize anyway. Forgive anyhow. What is it that you need to forgive yourself for?"

"For letting my children down. For not being enough. For letting myself down. For being the mom that I thought they expected me to be instead of the mom that they needed me to be. I sacrificed so much of what was important to me to give them everything I thought they needed and wanted."

Moon replied, "Parents often put their children's needs first and put their own needs on hold, feeling selfish if they take time for themselves or pursue their own dreams. They mistakenly dim their own light so that their children might shine brighter. Allowing the expectations of what a parent should be, and of what others think, to get in the way of living in balance. When evaluating the source of your light, are you coming from truth and unconditional love, or are you coming from Ego?"

I am the bow, not the Archer. "Maybe it is Ego that gets in the way. Needing them to fulfill my joy or dreams is not loving unconditionally. Instead, I must be strong, stable, and flexible to meet their needs. The arrow needs the bow, not the other way around. I am happy to be the bow. Still, I am afraid to let go."

"You can only begin to heal when you decide to let go," said Moon. "Do not attach to your pain or your fear—choosing to hold it allows you to continue to be affected by it. Let it go. Surrender. Call out the feeling and then set it free. We must embrace the darkness, this is where the work gets done. Where we find the things we hid away because we thought we could deal with them later. It is not the darkness that you fear, darkness is merely the absence of light, the light never goes away. So, what are you really afraid of?"

Moon knew there was a deeper truth causing my suffering. The words poured out of me, "I am afraid of rejection, being misunderstood, being alone. I am afraid of the 'what ifs' coming true. I am afraid of forgetting who I am and what I love."

"Recognizing your triggers, your mistakes, is how you grow. It's how the light returns. The goal is not to be perfect; the goal is to be the best version of yourself. Honoring your work and your progress is how you move into the light; shame and guilt serve no purpose here. They will only hold you back. Take nothing personally. It's not all about you. It is so much bigger than you. I wish you could see you from my vantage point. I see you. I hear you. I understand it feels real and personal from where you are sitting, and it's so easy to be defensive when you feel attacked."

"I obsessively replay the events that happened over and over in my mind, asking why, and trying to make sense of it all. I ponder how to survive if my worst fears come true."

"Trust the process. You don't need to have all the answers. You know enough. You *are* enough. We don't always have to understand the reasons for the pain or the grief, just maybe the experience is necessary. Imagine your painful experience is necessary for something glorious to manifest in someone else's life or even in your own future. Be grateful for the lessons, no matter how hard, because they become your story, they shape who you are. You may never know the reasons, but with love you can be brave and surrender, anyway. Surrendering is the faith that allows space for growth, and love creates space that allows others to grow too, as we are all connected."

I took a deep breath and made peace with the darkness. I called it by name. I closed my eyes and recognized that I had tucked other pain away—that also wanted to be seen and heard. For the first time in a long time, I recognized a part of myself that I had shut off from the world. There she was, sitting all alone in the dark. It was there in the darkness that the real healing began.

I explained to Moon my discovery: "For so long, I strived to be what everyone else wanted or needed me to be, and I lost sight of who I truly am. Doing things for others brings me joy, but striving to be a version of what others expect of me does the opposite, and often backfires, leaving me feeling misunderstood and rejected. I wonder why some people cannot see the real me—they pass judgment or think they know what I am going to say or how I'm going to react. And so often it is the opposite of what my heart truly feels or who I know I am inside. If they do not see the real me, then where does the problem lie, in their perception or in my presentation? Who am I presenting to the world? Why am I hiding the most beautiful parts of me?"

"Authenticity is about being honest with ourselves, honoring ourselves, and allowing all versions to be seen. Even our craters and our scars can be beautiful. Sometimes people choose to see only parts of us. We will never please everyone. Not everyone will like us or accept us. When we are authentic, we attract those who love us and see us for who we are, craters and all. Let your imperfections glow.

Authenticity is the connection to self, which allows us to feel empowered to shine. Allowing your light to shine starts with looking in the mirror and first accepting who you are, even the parts that feel broken and need work."

I expressed my doubt to Moon. "Could I honor myself enough to feel whole and connected? Could I still be the mother my children need me to be if I am not whole?"

"The moon is always whole, even if it is not full," Moon answered. "Sometimes we hide the most vulnerable parts of ourselves because we are not ready to shine in our full capacity. But that does not mean we are not *whole*, it just means we are not *full*. It is okay not to be full all the time. You can still rise and shine in whatever capacity you are capable of sharing. You don't have to wait to be full in order to shine. You deserve to be in love with your life right now."

I questioned Moon's authenticity, "What about your light? It is not your own, yet I marvel at your beauty and how you confidently light up the darkness."

Moon replied, "It is true that my light doesn't come from me; it's a reflection. It comes from Source. The light shines on me and I share that light with you, that is how we are connected. The light does not belong to us. Just as your children do not come from you and do not belong to you. We must not try to own it, hoard it, or capture it, we must share it; as we share our light, it grows brighter. Like the bow that sets the arrow in motion, light is a trajectory of Love. Love holds the power that heals. May gratitude fill your heart, and may your expectations be fluid and open to new possibilities and outcomes. The light is a gift that you give away. Wrap each of your children in light and love, and as you set them forth, know that you are always whole."

Like the moon and all of its phases, uncovering our light is not something we will do, it is something we work towards doing every day, in every cycle, in every season. It is the process. Trust the process.

Chapter 5
Let Light Guide You Home

Crystal MacGregor

"Life happens for us, not to us; although we may not see it that way at the time, our darkest moments can lead us to some of our greatest blessings and are often the catalyst we needed to awaken our truest self within."

Crystal is a food lover, registered dietitian, personal trainer, creative cook, lifelong learner, and dog mamma. Crystal believes that everything in life happens in our favor. Even though we often don't see it that way at the time, our darkest moments can lead us to some of our greatest blessings. We are all explorers on a unique journey to discover who we really are and what we are capable of, while finding our true purpose. We all have unique gifts deep inside that can positively affect the world. We just need to get out of our own way and let them shine. Crystal is grateful and humbled by the opportunity to be a contributing author in this book, amongst such a passionate group of women who radiate love and light. She hopes to inspire all who read this to live their best life. How we eat, move, think, and feel can have a great impact on our well-being. Life can throw curveballs, even appear to dim our light. Embracing a positive attitude, growth mindset, and learning from others strengthens us. It's time to step into our power, master our mind, raise our vibration, and unleash the light within.

crystalmacgregor.com

ig: cmacgregor ~ fb: crystal.macgregor

li: crystalmacgregor ~ t: CrysMacGregor

Daydreams. Sunbeams. Wonder.

Growing up in the countryside of rural Prince Edward Island, Canada was magical. Surrounded by beautiful rolling red clay tapestry, lush potato fields lined the perimeter of my family's home. The cool, crisp, salty ocean breeze kissed my face as I played in waves at the sandy beaches only a bike ride away from where I lived. I came from a family of humble blessings. We were taught that love, kindness, and happiness were all that really mattered in life. As the oldest child of four siblings, I was often known as the loud, curious, outgoing one, filled with hope, joy, and curiosity.

When traumatic events happened in life, my mom, wise beyond her years, told us that, "Life never gives you more than you can handle." I believed this, but didn't realize how much I would rely on it until much later in life.

I have wondered, How well do I know myself? Reality hit me hard when I realized I was a people-pleaser and struggled with setting boundaries. I felt drained. It was as though I somehow lost that childhood sparkle. I've always been an optimist, been grateful for whatever life put on my path, but something changed. Something felt off. I needed to evolve and grow, somehow find my true self. When you become more aware and choose to put yourself first, something magical happens. Every aspect of your life gets better. You learn to protect your most valuable asset—your energy.

Weathering Life's Storms

Life can throw some pretty big curveballs. I always seemed to have a plan, and like the ocean, I went with the flow. Have you ever experienced a time when what you thought you wanted ended up differing from what you actually needed?

Like a dark and rainy day, a storm was brewing when the global COVID-19 pandemic hit. I had just moved back to beautiful

Victoria, British Columbia after living throughout Canada for the previous decade. I was a military wife and grateful to have followed my husband's career, living in new places, meeting new people, and experiencing new things. My husband and I had purchased our new home, a light and airy penthouse with a wrap-around balcony overlooking a beautiful park. I'd had my eye on this property for years and could not believe that it became available with such divine timing. I couldn't have been happier, or so I thought.

I was finally going to work onsite with my amazing team after a decade of splitting my time between traveling and working virtually. I had travel plans lined up to celebrate big birthdays and to go back home to PEI to spend time with my family and friends. My husband was finally retiring after twenty years in the military. He had secured an airline job and would join me in Victoria a few months later. I would set up our home on my own.

I didn't know then, but 2020 would be a life-changing year. My life would be turned upside down. It would be the year when I had to face my biggest fears and some of my darkest times. This was the year when I lived on Pandora Avenue, in my fabulous new home, and it would be the year of opening Pandora's Box.

It was a challenging year as we all faced a global pandemic. Fear of the unknown crept in. I had never lived alone before, and this was the year I would experience solitude. In isolation, miles— and what felt like a lifetime—away from my family and friends, I worked from home instead of the office. The airlines slowed to a halt and my husband decided to stay in the military and not move to Victoria with me. I would live at Pandora by myself. This was going to be different. How would I cope? As an extrovert, this felt like my worst nightmare. I longed for connection. I remembered how, when I was scared as a child, I would crawl into bed with my sister and ask for her arm around me. She would hold me and I felt safe. I wished I had that then. I loved people, and I found myself calling home more often, spending hours on Facetime with friends near and far, and talking to strangers on balconies around me just to have a connection.

My relationship with my husband became turbulent. I needed to find courage and strength to keep moving forward. We often self-identify with our relationships. Eleven years of marriage felt like a long time. With a heavy heart, I knew it was time to break free and ended our marriage. I'd been living in a fog for years. Who was I? What did I really want in life? Who did I want to be? Asking questions of myself wasn't easy. At times, life's journey felt heavy and dark. But I always felt the light streaming in through the window onto my face as I sat on my living room floor, gazing out upon the beautiful park, wondering what my future would hold. Change is inevitable and can be hard at times. This felt scary! What was I going to do?

Fear and uncertainty lingered. I was in survival mode. As tears fell down my face, a little voice inside me whispered, "Life never gives you more than you can handle." I wiped away my tears and reminded myself that I had this. I received daily check-ins from friends and family. I was forever grateful as these were *my* people. You see, love knows no boundaries, and I could feel their strength from near and far. This kept me grounded. Then something magical happened. I remembered what it felt like to be me. The *real* me. The one who used to daydream, feel endless joy, and was filled with curiosity.

The fog lifted. It was time to learn, evolve, grow, and declutter my life from anything that did not serve my highest good. I committed. It was time to listen to my body and notice how I felt. Something shifted. I noticed that my energy felt different.

Thankfully, life always gives you what you need. I'd wanted a puppy for years, but traveling so much for work made it a challenge. During the pandemic, it was as though I manifested the perfect Frenchie, just for me. Months later, I took my pup, Bruno, home. It felt like the longest wait and it was love at first sight. Little did I know then that he would become one of my greatest teachers, showing me the value of unconditional love. He was my therapist, snuggle buddy, and brought so much laughter and joy when I needed it most.

Travel continued to be postponed. I missed seeing my friends and family as we celebrated special occasions, the birth of my two new nieces, and even Christmas, virtually. Christmas was the hardest. I missed my mom's potato dressing. I missed hugging my family and friends. I missed the hustle and bustle of it all. Gratefully, I had Bruno and incredible close friends in my "bubble."

A few months after Christmas, after living alone for a year, I had two weeks to find a new home. It felt overwhelming. I needed to sell, donate, and discard half of all my belongings and move again. I said goodbye to my Pandora home, took one last look at the beautiful park, and said hello to my freedom. I welcomed the unknown with open arms. This took courage, but I was ready. It was time. My friends and family had my back. The pandemic persisted, making it more challenging to find a new home. With luck on my side, Bruno and I found a charming place with a yard. You see, the Universe always has your back, too. I packed tirelessly as Bruno chased the rolls of packing tape. If only he could have packed boxes instead of pouncing on them. It was a busy weekend fueled by caffeine. Hope filled my heart. This was going to be a new chapter!

Moving Forward Meant Journeying Deep Within

Moving forward meant that 2020 would be the year I saw things crystal clear. It was the year I stepped back into my power and turned inward to find the answers I needed to evolve. My time at my Pandora home, alone, became my haven. Gratefully, it would be a quiet place to escape, come undone, and take refuge from the storm. This still felt scary, though, for an extrovert like me. I needed to be brave. I knew in my heart this was the right path for me and that it would be worth it in the end.

Along the way, I learned three lessons that changed my life forever, helping me feel more in alignment with who I was, how I was evolving, and who I was becoming. I hope they inspire you, too.

Lesson 1: Let It All Go

I had to take a moment and pause. I questioned everything—my goals, my values, and what felt good to me. What if there were no right or wrong answers? What if, instead, we could observe ourselves, others, and life experiences as they are, see them as neither right nor wrong, without judgment? What if instead, we could see them as opportunities to learn and grow? Sometimes we focus on the darkness we feel inside, the mistakes we feel we made along the way, instead of celebrating how far we've come, the progress we've made, and the light we embody. I learned we need to take 100% accountability for who we are, all of it, light and dark (the dark is painful, I know!). We need to embrace how incredible we are and how much we've grown. Set yourself free and let it all go! Forgive yourself, others, circumstances, and stop trying to control your journey—the past or future. Becoming more aware and simply observing your life and how you feel creates a powerful mindset. Awareness may feel heavy before it feels light. You have the power to choose to move through life freely, staying in the present moment. Once I did this, I felt lighter, happier, and more like me than I had in a long time.

Lesson 2: Tune In, Not Out

Use your internal compass, your heart. Remember what my mom told me: Life never gives you more than you can handle. It doesn't always feel that way, but I believe this is true. It's as though our bodies have a secret love language that speaks to us when we pause and pay attention to how we feel in our bodies when life events happen. Feel and listen. I like to think of this process as tuning in, not out. It might surprise you how often what we think doesn't always align with how we feel. Trust the feeling. Live in your body instead of your head.

Lesson 3: Choose Faith Over Fear

The unknown terrain can be scary and uncomfortable, especially when it takes us to unfamiliar places. But I've learned that's where the magic happens. Whenever we feel frightened, it is important to be still and breathe. This is crucial since it helps us stay present, and prevents us from spiraling into thinking about the future, or dwelling on the past. Breathing is life itself and has the power to ground us and to prevent our bodies and minds from going into flight, fight, or freeze (a.k.a. survival mode).

I was fortunate to have the time and space to pause and assess my life. This allowed me to become aware of what served me, brought me joy, and gave me energy, and what felt heavy and draining. I embraced vulnerability, looked fear in the face, and vowed to retain only what served my highest good. This aligned with feelings of joy, positivity, and love. I took 100% accountability for all that happened in my life. After my marriage ended, I started setting boundaries to protect my most valuable assets, my time, attention, and energy. This was my path of self-discovery and healing. No more making up stories in my mind of what I thought I needed, judging others, or assuming. It was time to live life unapologetically, as *me!* Embracing all that I am, noticing my energy, and how I feel.

It's time to get out of our own way and stop living like we are in survival mode. You see, we can get stuck in that place—I've been there. Instead, let's learn to embrace every thought and feeling as it comes, see it as it is, it's just energy. Let's think of this energy as an experience that is helping us evolve. I've also learned that it's important to hold in our mind what we want without expectation of exactly how we will get it. Instead, enjoy the journey. Breathing is powerful! You can take any energetic charges you feel in your body and imagine yourself hugging them on the inside, while awakening to the fact that everything happening in life is happening in our favor. This takes practice and over time, you'll discover you don't sweat the small stuff. This is how we level up our lives. Choose faith over fear, prayer over worry. Get out of your own way and feel the difference!

Light Can Guide Your Path Home

No matter how far you roam, your heart always knows its way back home. I ended up moving back to beautiful Prince Edward Island to be close to my family and friends. It felt so good to have the sun kiss my face, taste the salty air, feel the sand between my toes, and watch the waves crash upon the beach. Time seemed to stand still. It felt so good. This was always my destiny.

Life will always be full of ups and downs. How we view our journey determines how we choose to live life. We can embrace our journey with curiosity, authenticity, compassion, and joy, or feel lost in the shadows. No matter what is happening in life, we are just one decision away from choosing more love and joy and living our best life. You are so worth it!

I believe that life's journey is as unique as we are. Today we are exactly where we are meant to be in life, no further ahead or behind. Stop and breathe that in for a moment. Does this resonate? Why would we let anything or anyone hold us back from being all that we are meant to be? We are meant to shine brightly.

You are loved, powerful, and never alone. You get to decide who you truly are and who you are becoming. Our hearts know exactly what is best for us and what is really important. Trust that a higher power will show you the way to get there. Have compassion for yourself and others. We are all on a unique journey. Let light guide you home.

Chapter 6
From Pain to Purpose

Lesley James

"Sharing your stories of invisible illnesses empowers you to recognize that you are not alone. Discovering what makes you glow is the first step to living life fully, on your terms."

Lesley James (née Mogg) is a compassionate end of life planner, with a focus on protecting families by educating, supporting, and guiding them through important decisions during stressful times. Lesley started working as a Pre-Planning Advisor with Dignity Memorial after gaining her Funeral Pre-planner License through the Bereavement Authority of Ontario. Born to serve, educate, and empower others, she is also a licensed Willow EOL Educator™ and offers workshops remotely.

In 2020, Lesley made a career shift from the healthcare industry to the bereavement sector. She completed courses in end of life studies, hospice, palliative care, advance care planning, legacy, green burials, mental health first aid, death, dying, grief, and bereavement. Lesley volunteers as a regional co-representative at the Bereavement Ontario Network (BON), serving the regions of Simcoe-York-Dufferin. A Jamaican-born Canadian, Lesley lives just north of Toronto, Ontario and is proud of her wonderful adult daughter and son. In 2000, Lesley was diagnosed with Addison's disease, a rare autoimmune condition. In 2006, her son (age eight at the time) was diagnosed with Type 1 Diabetes.

Her core values are love, wisdom, and comfort. Lesley believes that: love softens grief, wisdom embraces fear, comfort soothes pain.

amazon.com/-/e/B096PR53JK

ig: lastwishesconsulting ~ fb: LastWishesConsulting

li: lesleyjames—lastwishesconsulting ~ t: lesley__james

Clubhouse: @lastwishes (Lesley James) ~ Goodreads: Lesley James

I didn't sign up for this! It was February 2017 and there I was, by myself, in the emergency department of my local hospital. Seated in a wheelchair, I held an emesis bag in one hand, and clutched my "emergency file" in the other. I was so weak and felt so sick. My forehead was pounding. I closed my eyes to avoid the bright lights, and wrapped my winter scarf over my throbbing eyelids. I felt nauseated and even though I thought I had nothing left inside me, I vomited again. I faintly begged for help, "Somebody, please. Help me. I have Addison's disease." I mustered up a bit of energy and waved my important documents. If only someone would read the papers that I had painstakingly assembled for this type of emergency.

You see, I was having my second Addisonian crisis, also known as an adrenal crisis, and felt like I had fallen head first into a deep, dark, and terrifying hole.

***

Like many of us, my world has been partially filled with shattered dreams, personal losses, some trauma, and, of course, grief. In May 2000, I was diagnosed with Addison's disease, a serious and rare autoimmune disease wherein the body does not produce cortisol.

Fight-or-Flight Stress Response

Cortisol is the primary stress hormone produced in the cortex, the outer part of the adrenal glands. Because I have Addison's disease, my cortex layer is damaged and does not produce cortisol, so I need to take the hormone orally in order to survive. Adrenaline production is unaffected, as it comes from the medulla, the inner part of the adrenal glands. You may have heard that when the body experiences stress, the fight-or-flight response is initiated, which triggers the release of adrenaline. In the twenty-two years I've lived with Addison's disease, I always chose "flight." I experienced my fair share of stressors, and too many over-reactions to stress. Sadly, my health became impaired due to the chronic activation of this survival mechanism and the imbalance of cortisol. For example, in March of 2020, at the start of the pandemic, self-preservation mode kicked in, which caused me to leave a full-time job.

I am sharing my story as it's my time to "fight," to be strong, build, cultivate, and nurture resiliency. Will it be easy? No. But, I now have the experience, wisdom, and determination to implement the coping strategies I've learned. I am tired of being tired.

Words Associated with My Pain

Abdominal, Burning, Chronic, Debilitating, Exhausting, Flare, Grimace, Hurts, Intense, Joints, Knotted, Limiting, Moderate, Nagging, Overwhelming, Persistent, Quality of Life, Relentless, Spoonie, Tender, Unbearable, Vulnerable, Widespread, X-cruciating, Yoga, Zebra.

Within two years of my first adrenal crisis in 2014, I was subsequently diagnosed with two other conditions: fibromyalgia and irritable bowel syndrome (IBS). Fibromyalgia is chronic, widespread pain, and I also experience "fibro-fog," which impacts my concentration, decision-making, and thought processes. With IBS, I experience pains in my stomach, digestive issues, constipation, and bloating.

Interesting Fact: Abdominal pain is a symptom of all three: Addison's disease, fibromyalgia, and IBS, so it's often tricky to determine how to treat.

Life with pain is difficult. Living with pain and without purpose is even harder.

Rare is Rare—Don't Compare

My diagnosis does not define me. I accept it, but prefer to remove the medical labels. Addison's disease, also known as Primary Adrenal Insufficiency, means that my body does not produce two critical hormones, cortisol and aldosterone. Of course, this is an over-simplification, since it is a very complex disease and often is present along with other auto-immune diseases. Patients with Addison's will need hormone replacement therapy for life. Chronically ill people are often told, "Oh, but you don't look sick." The reality is that no one sees your day-to-day struggles, as you appear "fine" from the outside. It's extremely important to avoid stress. This is not a competition you want to win. Avoid comparing Addison's disease to other rare diseases and invisible illnesses. I acknowledge that Addison's disease impacts every aspect of me physically, spiritually, holistically, practically, emotionally, financially, socially and mentally.

The Concept of Lantern Bearers

There were three events in July 2021 that sparked the idea for this part of my chapter. First, I came across a photo of my second cousin, a teenager at the time, as a proud torchbearer, leading up to the Canadian Winter Olympics in 2010. She carried the torch and its flame as she ran down Main Street Markham, close to where I live. Second, I reflected on the 22nd anniversary of my paternal grandmother's funeral in July 1999, in which I had the honor of being one of her pallbearers. This was a momentous occasion—she lived to be one hundred years old and her six granddaughters who lived in Toronto were her pallbearers. Third, I used a small, turquoise lantern to bring some added light to a family gathering as we sat in my backyard one evening. This reminded me of the days growing up in Jamaica when we lost electricity due to blackouts and my parents would bring out the kerosene lamps.

Thus, the idea of using "Lantern Bearers" to convey my story was born. Unlike pallbearers, you will not need these six individuals at the same time, nor in the same place. In fact, during a pandemic, some of them can be that beacon of hope from a distance. Similar to being selected as a torchbearer for The Olympic Games, it is considered to be a tremendous privilege to be chosen as a Lantern Bearer for a person living with an invisible illness.

Honorary Lantern Bearers are optional and, as in the case of honorary pallbearers at a funeral, there is no limit to the number you can have. I chose to have two additional people as honorary Lantern Bearers to ensure optimal social and mental well-being. Addison's disease is challenging, but it is not all doom and gloom. When I am feeling well, it is important to socialize to welcome a sense of normalcy.

Your Lantern Bearers will help move rocks out of your way, both figuratively and literally. When I separated from my partner, I felt like such a failure and wanted to crawl under a rock and disappear. Thankfully, after the shock, my family was incredibly supportive. They made me realize that I was still loved, accepted, and that I was not alone. Over time, I became resilient and gained the confidence to push the huge boulder of an obstacle aside and start over. Even if you trip over the odd stone, persevere as your Lantern Bearers guide you out of the shadows into light. They will help you navigate through the joy and sorrow, the gratitude and grief, the happy and sad, and the good and bad. Indeed, I certainly welcomed my Lantern Bearers as I transitioned from flight to fight, from victim to victor, and from pain to purpose.

How to Choose Your Lantern Bearers to Uncover Your Light

People living with chronic medical conditions need extra support from their communities. I will highlight six compassionate support roles, your six Lantern Bearers, which foster living life fully.

1. The Specialist is your health care provider who diagnoses and treats your physical body and medical conditions. In Canada, I was referred to an endocrinologist whose specialty is the endocrine system. This system contains eight hormone-secreting glands: the adrenal gland, hypothalamus, pancreas, parathyroid gland, pineal gland, pituitary gland, reproductive glands (ovaries and testes), and thyroid gland. I also have a very good rapport with my family physician who I see at least annually, and have appointments by phone as needed. Find a qualified and confident doctor; these professionals are trusted experts. Health is wealth, but the reality is that delays in diagnosis are common for rare diseases. Life gets tricky when doctors cannot find anything wrong. The decline is so gradual and symptoms may mimic those of other illnesses. One of the hardest things is that no one can appreciate your

frustration or suffering. You may feel like you are barely existing, when all you need is a glimmer of hope. The only way to describe what I was going through is to say that there was a hole in my gas tank—I couldn't keep my tank full, and the hole kept getting bigger until I was depleted of my fuel. The light in my lamp had faded gradually, and all my previous energy was replaced with extreme fatigue, immense exhaustion, and constant pain. Addison's disease is an invisible illness and is often misdiagnosed. When it finally comes, learn to accept your diagnosis and begin prescribed medication right away and you will start feeling better.

2. The Empath is a highly sensitive person (HSP) who invites support on a spiritual level, accepts specific requests, and treats you the way you want to be treated. The empath learns to understand your triggers and can explain the benefits of non-traditional options. Mindfulness practices may be offered and you will be showered with empathy. Personally, I am a social introvert, and get along well with kindred souls who explore alternative healing therapies. Transform your thinking, set your boundaries, and reject unsolicited feedback from naysayers. Find your passion and what makes your heart sing.

3. The Advocate will observe your health and be available to attend key medical appointments. Providing support from a holistic (person as a whole) perspective is needed, while keeping the priorities and wishes balanced. A helpful skill for an advocate to have is being an effective communicator for patient-centered care and decisions. An advocate will coach you on how to speak up for yourself. For example, it is your right to ask for accommodations in your workplace, a lesson that I have learned the hard way.

4. The Assistant adds creativity and fun to otherwise mundane and practical tasks. This person knows how to get things done. Do you know someone who steps into action,

makes a difference, and creates change through awareness and education? Identify this person to lead you to make your impact and make moments count. The assistant tends to be organized to help you order medication, manage lab results, and schedule appointments.

5. The Grief Buddy is an unbiased person who offers emotional support by sitting with you in your discomfort and listening to your concerns and complaints. This compassionate individual does not need to have any professional certifications. If you are newly diagnosed, you will benefit from having a companion with whom to share your grief. The skill needed is the ability to be nonjudgmental. Allow yourself to transform from bitterness into contentment. Your grief buddy will help you to name your trauma, feel the emotions, and integrate mourning activities. For example, when I write, I am distracted from my struggles and pain, so I am consciously aware that post-traumatic growth is taking place. Let the process evolve. To uncover your light, you first need to discover a way out of the darkness.

6. The Bookkeeper is a person who is good with numbers. You may consider a family member who can assist with financial aspects, such as budgeting for medical expenses. This person is a liaison with an accountant or the government for filing income tax and submitting applications. Confidentiality is required. The bills and paperwork may seem daunting, but continue to live your core values. Find the gifts—support groups are priceless gems. If you have adrenal insufficiency (primary or secondary), become a member of your local organization. In Canada, I highly recommend The Canadian Addison Society.

My Core Values

I work and volunteer in the bereavement sector, and am currently an end of life planner and educator. As a person living with a stress disorder, it is meaningful to help families take the stress out of planning a funeral or memorial service in advance. This type of work chose me. Being of service is also a way for me to heal from my grief. Finding my purpose brought me comfort; discovering meaningful and fulfilling work allowed for personal growth. It is critical to keep my lens focussed on my "why."

In the spring of 2020, I began a wonderful journey with Willow EOL (End Of Life) and enrolled in an amazing and life-changing personal development course. The online program is called 7 Tools for Making Sense of Life & Death and working through this course allows me to live my life with intention and purpose. It was truly transformative. As a result, I became a licensed Willow EOL Educator™, an experience that led me to develop my three core values, which are love, wisdom, and comfort. In my end of life studies, some common words that kept coming up were grief, fear, and pain, so I was extremely intentional in finalizing my values.

I believe that love softens grief.

Love—Unconditional love is critical to any relationship. I love deeply and will never be ashamed of how much I love or who I love. I know love never ends, even after the death of a loved one. When we experience a significant loss, the emotion we feel is called grief.

I believe that wisdom embraces fear.

Wisdom—I consider myself a lifelong learner. There is so much wisdom that has been passed down from our ancestors. I am grateful for the wise people in my life who are able to answer questions and lessen my worries, anxieties, and fears.

I believe that comfort soothes pain.

Comfort—I have witnessed family and friends who have suffered physically due to long terminal or age-related illnesses. Many also suffer emotionally, due to seeing their loved ones in discomfort. I have learned to get comfortable with uncomfortable conversations.

I follow the work of Dr. Elisabeth Kübler-Ross, a world-renowned psychiatrist, humanitarian, and hospice pioneer. Here is one of the famous quotes from this influential author in the field of death studies, palliative care, and grief support:

"People are like stained-glass windows. They sparkle and shine when the sun is out, but when the darkness sets in, their true beauty is revealed only if there is a light from within." -Elisabeth Kübler-Ross, M.D.

Whether you have been recently diagnosed with a rare disease or are currently living with an invisible illness, I want to support and comfort you in your journey. My hope is to empower you to love yourself first, feel comfortable embracing your inner wisdom, and be inspired to uncover your light.

Sending love. Sharing wisdom. Offering comfort.

Chapter 7
Prioritize Protecting Yourself

Sara Curleigh-Parsons

"Figure out the armor you need to shield and protect yourself, it comes in all shapes and sizes, and when it fits—keep it close, wear it, and use it!"

Canadian-born and worldly bred, Sara grew up with three spirited older brothers, a nurturing mother, and an insightful General as a father, so she needed to leave the comfort of home to find her own essence. Hours after accepting her honors degree from Bishop's University, a place she picked because she loved the color purple, she headed across the ocean to the UK. She discovered Europe by backpack, taught English in Slovakia, completed graduate work in southern France, and arrived in Belgium as a new bride, knowing nobody and without a job.

Adventure and curiosity sum up what Sara is all about. Thirty years and four children later, these qualities have shaped her life; they drew her to Europe and inspired her to build a thriving learning consultancy.

Sara has always pushed herself and felt at peace with the unknown. The events of the past few years have pressed Sara far beyond her comfort zone, but love of adventure and curiosity have ensured that she continues to learn. She has recalibrated and reinvented her business and learned to balance yin with yang, braving a paddleboard marathon, conquering the Vallee Blanche, and now excitingly embarking on a new adventure coauthoring a book.

ig: sara.curleigh.parsons ~ fb: Sara.Curleigh-Parsons

https://www.linkedin.com/in/saracurleighparsons/

Goodreads: Sara Curleigh-Parsons

"Sara, I'm so sorry to hear about you and Scott." Seriously, how does someone who I work with less-than-occasionally even know his name?

"What a shock to you. You must have been devastated. Did you really not know or even suspect?" Awkward pause. I give nothing away.

"And . . . you look so amazing and manage to keep working. I guess what doesn't kill you makes you stronger!"

What doesn't kill you makes you stronger? Seriously?

Just banish that thought from your mind, your mouth, your existence. I didn't want to almost die to become strong. I don't want or need to look over a cliff edge, shaking, wobbling, wanting to jump. It's not that I ever wanted to jump or even contemplated it. But for goodness sake, don't tell *me* that what will not kill me, will make me stronger.

The voice in my head is thankfully being supportive today. She says, *Don't engage with them. Focus on prep for the next session of your workshop.* I turn my back and stand tall in my red high heels, grounding myself with a deep breath in, and a long, calming breath out. I will ignore them.

What have I learned from going through trauma? That I need to find a way to protect myself. That pushing back takes too much energy sometimes. That trying to have a clever word or phrase to use as rebuttal, or pretending to be fine when I'm not, is just too darn hard. That I don't want to push back; I don't want trauma to touch me in the first place.

Instead, I figured out that I needed to have armor, my own coat of arms, a Teflon shield that could protect my insides, my broken heart, and my exploding brain. I needed something to help me heal instead of letting more arrows plunge into me.

Figure Out Your Armor

- Know when to tune out. Make metaphorical earplugs.
- Put in boundaries. Build walls where required.
- Don't dissect the past. Avoid looking over your shoulder.

Know When to Tune Out

Trauma is real and terrifying when you are the victim. As a sympathetic outsider, you can feel helpless in your capacity to support, placate, or comment. It can feel like saying nothing is taboo. Rest assured, saying nothing is much better than uttering something that can hurt, degrade, or minimize.

Being told things like, "What doesn't kill you makes you stronger," has the same effect as saying *suck it up*. At first, when this was thrown at me like a bone, I would smile and swallow hard and find a way to peel myself away from the potentially well-meaning, but more likely unthinking, person. What I learned was to not allow those people near me in the first place—not to let careless arrows find me, intentionally aimed or otherwise.

And, saying, "It must be so hard and lonely being in that big house by yourself," is also unhelpful. I was solid in my belief that my marriage didn't define me; I was not defined by my husband, despite what many wanted me to believe. Their thoughts were not fact. He was my best friend, my soulmate, my lover, the father of my children, the person I've laughed and cried with more than anyone else, but I never wanted him to define me. He was part of me, like a limb, like something that sometimes hurts me, makes me tingle, is useful, and is always there. It felt beyond comprehension not having him to turn to for advice on how to handle the explosion in my life, along with the comments, smirks, whispers, and eye-contact-avoidance I was now facing. But I was not lonely, rattling around in the home we had built for our forever.

Tip: Don't let people's opinions become your facts!

In my workshops, I encourage people to focus on the objective of their communication. I ask them to reflect upon and then decide what they want as a result of what they are saying. When they give feedback, what do they want to see done differently or better? This is a life lesson.

The advice goes both ways—from the person speaking and the person receiving. Start from a place of understanding not judging. Please don't judge me and I will try hard to not judge you.

"Sara, I am so shocked to hear about you and Scott. I mean, I am in my marriage for life, everyone has issues, you don't just give up . . ." Who is this for? I took this as a direct hit to me, in hindsight it was her issue not mine but it was incredibly painful at the time.

After my separation, when random people gossiped to me about someone's marriage troubles, or shared their catty comments or offhand remarks, my stomach would curdle. These conversations were happening around me, and about me, no doubt. It was gut-wrenching. My real friends allowed me to cry and made me laugh.

Decide what kind of communication you're willing to engage in—if it hurts you, don't even listen to it.

Tip: Add earplugs to your armor.

Put In Boundaries

At work, I had clear boundaries. The upside of being a consultant was that nobody knew what was going on in my life. Many times, my eyes welled up during a Resilience for Leadership workshop, while I professed to be an expert to the group in front of me, stressing to them to put their own oxygen mask on first. I needed to remind myself as much as others. The problem was, the oxygen was sucked out of me so much, I could barely breathe. When pain is so close, it's tough to realize that you can help yourself. I reflected on what calmed me and helped me focus, and I prioritized these things. Whether it was soaking in the bath, breathing in the lavender oil that drenched my skin, or stopping on the way home to fully take in the majestic views that working in London afforded me, or pondering how I added value to those I worked with that day, I always chose to concentrate on what allowed me to refocus my lens. This was a helpful reminder that I needed to be my own biggest cheerleader, that micro-techniques work, and resilience is about bouncing forward.

A recurring theme built up—the more resilient I got, the more people thought it was just my natural self, that I didn't have to work hard at it, every hour of every day. It is true that resilient people often appear unscathed, they make it look easy. It wasn't that people didn't think I was resilient, they didn't know the depth of the reason I needed to be.

"Sara, you make resilience sound easy. Your life is together, you don't drop any balls, and you're so focused. How can you really understand trauma?"

It was an obvious and fair question, but one I wasn't prepared to answer. Boundaries at work were armor for me. Deep breath in for four, out for four, and again.

I wanted to say, "You would gasp if I told you what I am going through daily." Instead, I openly shared my mantra, taken from Sheryl Sandberg: "I am more vulnerable than I thought, but stronger than I ever imagined." This became my go-to phrase when I headed down an unwanted path.

And I didn't say that, for hours the night before, my soon-to-be ex-husband and I sat stiff, hand-in-hand on the sofa, discussing our incomprehensible situation. His armor was always to be the fun guy, telling entertaining tales and embellishing stories to get laughs. He was loved by so many, and how difficult it must have been for him, wondering whether he was ever loved for who he truly was. That same question appeared on my ever-developing reel of pain. Was I loved for me, or for who he needed me to be, the person who provided a family and concealed his reality? He once joked about his own family.

"Wouldn't it be funny if they called here, and you just said I didn't live here anymore? That would show them." He laughed at himself.

And I cried. It wasn't funny. This was my life, the life he was pulling apart, derailing, shredding, and I couldn't see the funny side.

He didn't know his boundaries, so I found it hard to define mine. I should not have waited.

Tip: Be Proactive with Your Boundaries!

He couldn't decide when to move out. He had sorted out a new flat, but the final step was like walking in treacle, as the Brits say, or walking in molasses, as the Canadian part of me understands it. We had been invited on a luxury skiing trip to a best friend's incredible chalet with four other families. He didn't want to tell the kids until after the ski trip, saying, and these words still make my blood boil, "I don't want to miss a family holiday."

I was incredulous, took a deep breath, and forced myself to say, "You are going to miss all the family holidays because we aren't a family anymore. You are tearing it apart."

Why did I have to point out the obvious? This was killing me, and I didn't need to create any more battles to fight, that's for sure! My armor was non-existent at that point. I was completely raw.

It was hard not to orchestrate everything. I sought help and guidance on how to tell the children; he was too caught up in his world to think his way might not be the right way. I did put up *that* boundary. I decided it was his decision to leave, so he needed to tell the kids.

It was a haunting moment when he said, "Mom and I aren't happy . . ."

Deep breath. I cut him off and said, "No, that's not true. I was happy."

The problem was that my needs were so dramatically over-shadowed by his. He had insisted that I didn't tell anyone the reason we were separating because he wasn't even sure. But he did know, by his own admission, he had met his boyfriend months before. Turning his life upside-down and knowingly causing pain for our children was never a decision he would have taken lightly. Back then, his focus was being a family man—he loved our children more than anything in the world. In holding back his explanation for leaving, I wanted to believe he was trying not to hurt anyone; however, history tells me it's more likely he didn't want to be the bad guy, the reason for the carnage. Perhaps he wasn't strong enough to handle it, but that did not mean I was. I knew the truth and being forced to mislead my children made me feel helpless. I wanted to be able to say I had been honest all the way—but I was caught in his emotional tug of war. His boundary felt so large and solid, like his six-foot-four-inch, two hundred pound frame. I didn't consider for a moment that I could question it. There was absolutely no playbook.

I felt humiliated that my marriage was breaking down and guilty for what I was doing to our amazing kids, even though it was none of my doing. He wanted to open up to the children in his own time, but that moment didn't come until eight months later, drip feeding the truth to our four children, one by one, over six long de-stabilizing weeks, insisting that he couldn't find the time.

I can say hand on heart, I didn't judge his sexuality and I was proud of my kids for not judging him either, the issue was—there was never a clear reason for the children as to why he left. It would have made so much sense, been easier to reconcile and answered so many questions. Questions I was left to field and deflect. But I knew he couldn't, he wasn't able, and I supported him with that. Our separation therapist acknowledged that although he would be revered by his new community, held up on a pedestal and told how brave he was, I would go through a trauma like nothing I was prepared for, while having to keep family life going strong. He agreed in principle, although he could not seem to link his actions to my trauma. I gave him space and encouraged him to explore his life while we both wore masks, hiding our reality every day. His mask was chosen, mine was forced.

Define and create boundaries for yourself, for your ex, for your friends, decide what *you* need, not what they need.

Tip: Build walls where required.

Don't Try to Dissect the Past

We all waste precious time and unnecessary energy asking questions that will never be answered. For me, I asked myself if I made him gay? As I write this, it sounds ridiculous, and hopefully as you read it, you are laughing. But this thought seeped into my mind daily, like hearing the constant drip drip drip of a tap not quite shut off, no matter how forcefully I turned it. Extraordinary, constant pain.

How did I not know? I sought every opportunity to examine what I'd missed. I never asked myself why it mattered. My anxiety was about unreasonable behavior, not sexuality.

The label didn't matter to me, but it did to others. Near strangers would ask probing questions about our intimacy. These questions bring me back to moments in time and my mind sticks, ponders, mulls, dissects . . . like quicksand sucking me in. I curse my amazing memory.

This is where I needed boundaries and earplugs and had none. I know now that it was unhelpful to engage in these crushing conversations, but I thought maybe someone else had an answer I couldn't find.

Tip: Don't get tangled in exploration with people who know less than you do.

I don't remember when I realized things weren't right. I guess it was when I acknowledged that feeling in the pit of my stomach, the one that told me we could not go on with so much in our relationship that was unknown. I delayed bringing up my concerns, thinking instead that my best friend and soulmate would open up, that he would give me the truth. Or, if not the truth, an acknowledgment that something needed carrying to the center of the room. Had he tried? Had I failed to notice? In my journals I detailed so many scenarios where I should have picked up clues, where others profess to have seen something obvious, but without the emotional entanglements, it is unquestionably clearer. Be kind to yourself. It is only in retrospect things become obvious. In the moment, they are events, like the millions of others that make up any marriage. It is easy to feel like a complete idiot or a fool when broken hearted but that serves no purpose. I simply didn't know, and when I finally confronted him on that warm June day, I know now that my heart broke, but did not shatter irrevocably.

Tip: Avoid looking over your shoulder.

I don't need to be reminded again about what happened next, how it changed my world, how he stood up for me and our kids one minute and transgressed the next. Choosing to live in the painful memories of should've, would've, could've, is not valuable.

My armor is taking care of those arrows now. They will not find their way to me anymore. I have learned that the strongest protection and most comfortable armor comes from realizing I don't need to protect myself any longer.

Learn from me and discover how to bounce forward. Recognise that you need armor, and then make it. Know when to tune out, build boundaries, and don't dissect the past.

Chapter 8
You Do Matter!

Janet H. Lau

"There may be times you feel small, limited, and unworthy. Your superpower is the ability to overcome such debilitating feelings while becoming more resilient and resourceful through your struggles. Know that you are a worthy and beautiful warrior. Know and trust that you do matter!"

Janet H. Lau works in a trauma hospital as a Medical Laboratory Technologist. She is a proud mother of her resilient daughter and together they strive to break through social expectations of normalcy. Janet relishes the different hats she wears in life: a mother, a sister, a friend, a healthcare worker, a teacher, a volunteer, an author, and a strong, independent woman.

As someone who struggled with self-esteem issues, and as the author of *The Little Grey Pig*, Janet actively encourages the building of children's self-confidence and reminds everyone of the importance of believing in themselves. These are essential building blocks in formulating a positive perception of oneself. With a passion for teaching, Janet actively promotes the importance of teaching with patience and love. She wholeheartedly believes that everyone needs a safe space to explore their curiosities, ask questions, and make mistakes freely. By doing so, people, especially kids, can grow up more confident and better equipped to navigate through their mistakes. Through her journey in self-discovery, Janet uses her writing in hopes of helping empower others, as well as for her self-healing.

ig: littlehandsriri ~ fb: Janet H. Lau

li: www.linkedin.com/in/JanetHLau ~ t: littlehandsriri

Goodreads: goodreads.com/janethlau

What is motherhood? Motherhood represents various things to different people. For me, it signifies hope, the discovery of my inner strength, and acknowledging my true worth. Even though the success of motherhood isn't measured linearly or by any one entity, and being a parent is exhausting, I have learned to be vocal and self-empowered since becoming a mom. In addition to the physical skills I learned while raising my daughter, motherhood pushed me into becoming more self-aware, learning to draw boundaries, and being emotionally present for myself and others. These were traits and skills that I lacked before becoming a parent.

My past was composed of different layers of self-doubt, grief, and trauma from my childhood into adulthood. Some causes were beyond my control, and they wreaked havoc on my mental health. Other times, I was bombarded with constant reminders that I was flawed, that my life was of no value, and those closest to me often mocked my intelligence. Unable to escape my volatile surroundings, I accepted all the shaming and ridicule as "truths." My perception that I was a failure, and the deterioration of my sense of worth, threw me into depression during my high school years and intensified immensely during my adult years. The entangled emotional hardships and the constant belittling I experienced caused me to internalize the devaluation of my being and made me believe it was justifiable. I started questioning the purpose of my life and occasionally wondered if it was something worth continuing. My insecurities made me very naïve in relationships, and my rebellious attempts to stave off feelings of worthlessness were unhealthy. It was on my journey through motherhood that I realized even though you can't always change the behavior of toxic people or even your surroundings, you can change your perspective to one that is more positive, nurturing, and self-accepting. This necessary mental shift helped me realize I am *worth* more, that I do *deserve* more, and that I *am* more than I had previously believed.

Since I can remember, I have wanted to be a mother; however, it was difficult to attain. It involved a few miscarriages and a lot of heartaches. My daughter, Riley, eventually, miraculously, and unexpectedly came into my life. Near the end of my high-risk pregnancy, an inexcusable betrayal caused a huge upheaval in my life and tore my world apart. I still remember clutching onto my pregnant belly, crying uncontrollably that night. It was the sudden belly cramps that stopped my crying immediately, and my heart clenched from fearing that my pregnancy was in jeopardy. I decided to forgive what was unforgivable for the sake of my unborn child. Despite whatever I was feeling or going through, one thing was certain: As a soon-to-be-mother, I knew at my core that I wanted to be a strong role model for Riley and to help her establish a positive sense of self. I did not want her growing up despising herself, feeling less than, and believing that she was undeserving, as I had felt for most of my life.

The first four months of postpartum were cataclysmic to my mental health. I was facing the after-effects of an unplanned C-section, a colicky newborn, and severe postpartum depression. The onset of intense feelings of anger and grief blindsided me, feelings from my past that I thought had been put aside and forgotten. Looking back, it wasn't the betrayal that broke me, but rather its confirmation of my internalized belief that I was undeserving and worthless. Blame it on the exhaustion of being a new mother, or the inability to deal with any further psychological trauma, but I was suddenly very attuned to the embodiment of all the pain, darkness, and resentment that I had carried all those years. I felt asphyxiated and mentally depleted. I was crying one night while cradling my wailing newborn, attempting to soothe her. I kept apologizing to her for being a bad mother and putting her in an unfair and lacking situation. I apologized to her for not knowing what to do. I felt so utterly alone and lost in the current turbulence of my life. At that moment, I questioned the value of my continued existence, and yet, strangely, a small spark lit within me at the same time. Knowing that I was responsible for the life of this newborn ignited an inner strength that had always resided within me, however dormant. With it came the realization that I did matter somehow. Staring down at my daughter's face, I felt a desire to shed my unhealthy perception of "self," as well as purge the toxicity from my life. I realized not only did I want to be present every day in her life, but I was motivated to be a stronger person because of her. I was adamant in following my core values as a mother, which included: loving my child unconditionally; ensuring that she felt safe and wanted; teaching through encouragement rather than through shaming or intimidation; creating trust; providing support when needed; sharing the knowledge that mistakes can be learning opportunities and she won't be obtrusively reprimanded for them. I wanted her to know that I would always be there to guide her when she feels lost or is struggling, and that I would value and respect her individuality.

Unfortunately, life was a blur for the next little while. There was just too much destructive "noise" within my head and toxicity surrounding us during my marital transition. My state of mind was already in a daze as I now grappled with breastfeeding. My inability to successfully breastfeed was mentally exhausting. Internalized beliefs of self-inadequacy resurfaced and told me I was a failure in the basics of motherhood. The self-ridicule affected my psyche the most. After months of contemplation and countless failures to successfully breastfeed, I decided to fully switch to baby formula. Over time, I witnessed my happy baby thriving beautifully, which dissipated whatever fears I'd had. The experience brought about an awareness that every family's needs and processes will differ, depending on time, space, and situation. I wasn't a failing mother for choosing an alternative approach in caring for my child. In prioritizing my mental health as a person, it enabled me to function better as a mother overall. I realized it was okay not to follow the "ideals" written in parenting books, advised on the internet, or imposed by those close to me. I gradually learned to take deep breaths, to center myself, and to do what was best for my daughter and me as a family.

Aside from this one triumph as a new mother, I still struggled in navigating between my turbulent emotional life and simple daily tasks relating to my newborn. When I wasn't drowning in self-anguish, I had severe anxiety, worried I might drop the baby during bath time, or screw up changing a simple diaper. My first outing with Riley was nerve-wracking because of all the "what if" scenarios that kept looping in my head as I gathered more and more things for us to bring. I was catapulted into this catastrophizing fear that I would be blamed for any negative effects on my daughter's overall well-being, which could be caused by even one forgotten item, and condemn me to the category of negligent and bad mother. I was shouldering such worries while fighting to open up my clunky stroller. Having finally put Riley into her stroller, I began our walk, only to realize that I had forgotten my keys, cell phone, and purse. I screamed out in absolute frustration while marching back into the house, thinking we would never get past our front door. Despite this mentally draining experience, I continued working hard to prove that I could succeed as a capable parent and to avoid the often condescending stereotypes of being a single mother.

For me, being my own harsh critic and listening to the naysaying of others was easy, but being my own cheerleader took hard work. I adjusted to life with a baby by actively taking on various daily tasks in and out of the house with Riley strapped to me in her carrier. My confidence grew, and I reminded myself to laugh off any blunders that might occur. As parents, especially single parents, we are forever learning new lessons, and sometimes it can feel like a lonely journey. Know that you are never truly alone ... after all, we parents need to stick together and form our own village for support, right? Remember that while you are on your passage through parenthood, it is normal to stumble along the way, and even to fall flat on your face sometimes. Be kind, generous, and forgiving of yourself. Remember to breathe and enjoy every little moment with your child.

Although I was starting to enjoy motherhood, halfway into my maternity leave, I found my days were becoming monotonous and blurring into one another. I was losing touch with myself and constantly had brain fog. I was exhausted and felt lonely being left with my child all day, defeated by house chores, and irritated that my house was a never-ending mess, despite my efforts to tidy up. I was now in survival mode.

My depression was worsening as I trudged through each day mindlessly. Motivated by frustration and love, I registered Riley and me for story time sessions at the local library, a mommy and baby boot camp class, and most importantly, I took a deep breath and sought professional help for my mental state.

I started telling a stranger everything I had suffered in my life and the traumatic events that had happened in the past several months. I remember this stranger complimenting me on what a strong individual I was for braving through all these things. I sarcastically laughed in her face and replied, "I'm not strong . . . I'm just too stupid to know any better, and probably crazy." In hindsight, it was my strength and desire for a better life that helped me endure all that had happened to me. I felt lighter having unloaded my grief onto someone, but I was coming to her with decades worth of issues and unreasonably expected her to "fix me" in just a few therapy sessions. Besides lacking time and money to maintain these sessions, I also realized that nothing was going to change for the better unless I overcame my subconscious unwillingness to accept that the debilitating internalized "truths" were, in fact, false.

One of the hardest and most terrifying things I have ever done was taking a step back and reevaluating the "truths" about myself. It was through continuous self-reminders of my strengths and positive attributes that I was able to discern the lies from the truths in my distorted self-perception. I learned that while my emotional and psychological scars are a part of me, they do not define me. I realized they were reminders of what I had been through and how far I'd come.

My daughter's presence further inspired my road to healing and personal growth, but, like many things, it was a learning curve filled with tiny revelations. The first revelation was my ability to multitask in creative and fun ways when encountering potentially stressful situations. To overcome feeling isolated, I enjoyed playing loud music while doing various things around the house, and Riley was busy bouncing her diapered-bum around and dancing. We enjoyed our lunches picnic-style outdoors, and I soaked up some quiet time on walks while Riley slept in the stroller. More and more, I felt emotionally stronger, more confident, and happier. I acquired new hobbies, learned new skills, managed my time better, and eventually found my groove. I learned to let certain things slide and not worry needlessly about the little things.

I am a work in progress, and the bad thoughts didn't just magically disappear. It would be a lie to think so. Knowing that life is never stagnant and continues on indiscriminately, I focus on the footprints I leave behind in this life. Reflecting on the past few years, I have grown as an individual, a woman, and a mother. One thing's for sure: my reflexes are a lot faster now, (e.g., catching a falling cup, a thrown dirty diaper, and of course, my daughter saying, "Catch me mommy!" as she leaps from the top of the stairs thinking it's so funny). But in all seriousness, where my internal light was once almost snuffed out, it now shines much brighter because I know I am capable, worthy, and a fighter. I've learned to create, share, and listen with an open mind. I pride myself on my ability to not only work hard, but to work smart while multitasking and to simultaneously find time to have fun and enjoy life.

Having better clarity on myself, I now know that if I detect anything lacking in my life, I can trust that this lack is real, and I can also approach it without judgment. I will then work hard to improve the inadequacy. I refuse to let others dictate the value of my life. I won't permit anyone to imprison my individual growth through gaslighting, or to make me feel small and unworthy. Through the strength and brightness of my being, my daughter will grow up confident and emotionally healthy, qualities that she can perpetuate to those around her. I forgive those who hurt me, and I forgive myself for the many years of self-hatred. I remember that the benchmark for being a "good parent" isn't defined by others, but is a relationship between me and my child. No matter what your past or present is, no matter how imperfect you perceive yourself to be, or how insignificant you feel, know that *you do matter*. Use your past pains as a gauge for what life should be. Love each of your imperfections, and if you feel insignificant, then roar with all the pent-up passion within yourself so you can feel big. *Love* yourself, *value* yourself, and be *kind* to yourself.

My message to you, Dear Reader, and to my daughter, is this: Never keep hate in the heart because such negativity is toxic. Remember to always communicate. The fear, shame, and uncertainty that we bottle up inside ourselves are detrimental to our psyche. Focus on the abundance in your life. Learn to work with your hands, your voice, and your mind. Know that you learn and grow not only through surviving your past pains but through rejoicing in the wonders of each day, laughing with loved ones, and being kind to yourself. While we can still be cynics at times, know that you will feel lighter and more resilient when you focus on the good that the universe provides, no matter how small it may seem. I hope you thrive on the idea that you can do some good in the world and that it brings you joy to make a positive impact on someone's life. Look forward to each day, not because you are bracing yourself for what will come at you, but because you can't wait to see what happiness and enlightenment it will bring. Value your authentic self always, especially when you feel hindered, and stay true to yourself. Lastly, remember that while you are searching externally in the world for strength to succeed, some form of this strength already resides within you. Have the courage to dig deep and find it to rise and shine again.

Forever grateful,

-Janet (mom)

Chapter 9
Take Flight

Ada S. Lau

"Is the glass half-full or half-empty? What if it can be seen as completely full? The seemingly empty space comprises endless possibilities and potential for our future. When we adjust our perspective, we can see the world in a new light."

Ada is a lifelong learner whose curiosity drives her to explore the world around her. Her career path took a drastic turn when she left engineering to delve into the field of social service work. She has since dedicated her time to providing emotional and spiritual support to those with lived experience of schizophrenia, anxiety, depression, and dementia. Ada currently works in the social sector advocating for families and individuals with developmental disabilities and mental illnesses.

Ada's personal quest toward self-discovery and acceptance has motivated her to collaborate with other women in overcoming their fears and self-doubts. Her dream is to empower individuals to discover who they are, realize their true potential, and experience freedom. She believes everyone has a unique story to tell, wisdom to share, and a positive impact they can make in this world.

ig: ada.s.wong.7 ~ fb: ada.s.wong.7

li: linkedin.com/in/ada-lau-89175774

In the summer of '98, my siblings and I were returning from a family reunion when our hour-and-a-half lay-over at the Los Angeles airport compressed into twenty minutes. I remember dashing madly from end to end of one of the world's busiest airports with our oversized luggage in tow. It felt as though we were competing in a marathon as we weaved through a sea of tired travelers, dragging over fifty pounds behind us. We crossed the finish line and arrived in the knick of time to collect our prize: economy seats to home, sweet home.

Life can sometimes feel like a race. In our pursuit of happiness, love, success, wealth, or knowledge, we encounter obstacles of all sizes while carrying our personal luggage. I am the kind of traveler who packs for all occasions and is an expert at stuffing my suitcase to its maximum capacity. Even on a daily basis, I would pack an extra sweater, candies, bandaids, and a folding umbrella in my bag—just in case. Ironically, I had also packed excess luggage in my internal life as a result of not filtering out the expectations of others. Perhaps my trusting nature believed in the opinions of others more than my own. I also acquired memorabilia such as rejection, fear, and self-doubt from some of my more challenging life experiences. These extra weights gradually wore me down and I couldn't freely be myself. It took much time and effort to unload some of the unwant-ed items and replace them with lighter contents such as acceptance, joy, and self-love.

What's in a Name?

Growing up, my peers gave me many unsolicited labels: random, smart, chubby, funny, weird . . . to name a few. Looking back, the teasing and name-calling were not malicious and some were said in passing, yet they left a mark on my heart and I inadver-tently carried them with me into my adulthood. Words are powerful and, if misused or misinterpreted, can shape our self-perception and chip away at our self-esteem. For me, "smart but lazy" was a label that I internalized, one that stayed with me for years.

Being an immigrant from Hong Kong, the cultural expectation to be smart and get good grades in school was ingrained from a young age. As the youngest, I couldn't help but compare myself to my older siblings and attempted, in vain, to catch up to their outstanding academic achievements. In high school, I maintained good grades even though I had poor time management skills and lacked self-discipline in my studies. My friends knew me as a chronic procrastinator who only put in effort at the eleventh hour. If I obtained a less than desirable result, I would always have the excuse that I just didn't have enough time. Back then, I didn't realize that I was protecting myself from failure. I was afraid that if I tried my absolute best and gave myself ample time and still fell short of an A plus, it would mean that I wasn't smart enough or that I didn't measure up to others. Hence, I shied away from working hard because being smart and obtaining perfect grades was unattainable. Being labeled "smart but lazy" was more palatable than being called "not good enough." I now recognize that a fixed mindset limited me—the belief that one's intelligence, basic abilities, and talent are static and unchangeable.

Fear can cause us to live half-heartedly.

Emerging Patterns

There are often patterns outside of our awareness that influence our thoughts and shape our beliefs. I am the youngest of three and, oddly enough, I was always in multiple friend trios from kindergarten all the way to my university days. My best friends came in pairs and I appreciated I did not have just one, but two best friends. However, these best friends always seemed more close-knit with each other and excluded me from certain activities; the feeling of being left out became all too familiar. This repeated pattern impressed upon me the notion that I am "less than" and an unworthy friend.

Unbeknownst to me, this narrative was sewn into my mind at the tender age of eleven when my dad passed away unexpectedly from cancer a year after we arrived in Canada. My family and I did not know how to process the overwhelming grief, but managed to survive through a whirlwind of emotions. We coped as best as we could without the strong pillar of our family there to lean on. Logically, I understood my dad succumbed to cancer and was taken from us. I knew without a doubt that he loved us to the moon and back and would have done anything in his power to conquer the disease and see us grow up. Despite the circumstance, the fact was that he left and abandoned us prematurely (even though it was out of his control). Little did I know that a vicious lie began to brew in my mind at this vulnerable time: "I was not good enough for my dad to stick around and remain by my side." The trauma of losing my dad reinforced the thoughts that, "I am rejected and I am not worthy of love."

At a Crossroad

A few years later, I was seventeen years old and had to choose a career path, despite the fact that I had a limited understanding of myself and of the world. Initially, social work was my top pick, but I pushed aside the idea since it didn't guarantee a good income. Instead, I studied mechanical engineering because a brief career assessment indicated that I should consider a path related to math and science. Admittedly, I am intrigued by the idea of how things worked and I attempted to start various DIY projects to build or fix objects around the house. Naturally, engineering seemed to be a good fit. Moreover, I figured it would provide me with a stable future and a respectable status in society. I was secretly hoping that a professional title would conceal my inadequacies on the inside.

In my university career, I continued to master the art of procrastination. I often buried my head in my textbooks in the library. By that I mean I fell asleep on top of my readings and assignments. After graduation, I took the first job offered to me, working at an engineering company, so that I could save up to travel the world and daydream about becoming a food critic. The novelty of starting my career as an engineer was short-lived, and soon I was doing just enough to get through the workdays. I became increasingly dispirited and unmotivated, enduring a job that was incompatible with my personality and interests. I am a relational person who enjoys talking with people, yet I was working a job that required sitting in front of a computer all day with minimal human interactions. Deep inside, social work still called out to me. I was reminded how engaged I had felt while volunteering with those in need. I felt most alive when connecting with individuals, whether I was lending an ear to a friend, helping at homeless shelters in downtown Toronto, or venturing into remote villages in Uganda.

Despite being fully aware that I was in the wrong profession, I feared making any changes. I attempted to tolerate it while I figured myself out, but as life would have it, I was fired from my job. My engineer title and the status it provided, was taken away abruptly, so I questioned my abilities and who I really was.

Self-Worth

In the months following, I sorted through a multitude of emotions caused by the job loss—feelings of guilt, shame, anxiety, and confusion. I felt ashamed whenever I introduced myself to new people and had no answer to the simple question, "What do you do for a living?"

Although I did not enjoy working as an engineer, I clung to the professional identity, and it became my crutch. The removal of this facade exposed my internal beliefs that I was unworthy and not good enough. I was prone to being self-critical and struggled to accept compliments and affirmations, since they didn't align with my negative self-perception.

Unintentionally, I regarded academic achievement, occupation, and salary as a measure of my self-worth. This happened because I never took the time to take an inventory of my qualities and abilities, and to accept myself.

Change of Mindset

From time to time, life nudges us toward examining our perspective—to see things from a different angle. A tiny ant can look intimidating when it sits on top of your nose. Fear works similarly in that it can elicit fight, flight or freeze responses, which can incapacitate us and trick us into thinking that something is much bigger or more terrifying than it is. Elbert Hubbard said that, "The greatest mistake you can make in life is to be continually fearing you will make one."

My insecurities and critical inner voice blocked me from seeing past my situation and noticing the opportunities ahead. If I had kept my job, I would have spent years of my life feeling unfulfilled. I've since learned from the work of psychologist Carol Dweck about the importance of cultivating a growth mindset, which entails viewing mistakes and failures as opportunities to grow. Our natural abilities are merely our starting points, and diligence, a positive attitude, and the capacity to embrace changes or challenges are what will ultimately bring us to our desired destination. I was dissatisfied with the status quo—getting by and not living up to my potential. I was curious and yearned to see what I could accomplish if I applied myself. My turning point came when I finally took responsibility for my own actions and acknowledged that my poor work ethic needed to be addressed. I began to change my mindset and adjusted my behaviors, which included accepting my weaknesses and leaning into my strengths. I refused to be held back by fear and laziness. It was essential for me to re-evaluate myself, embrace new challenges, and start putting in the hard work.

Inner Healing

One of the best decisions I ever made was when I mustered up the courage to seek out counseling. My counselor helped me identify the root of my negative thought patterns, which enabled me to see how my experiences influenced not only my thoughts but also my behaviors and emotions. Patterns of rejection had transformed over time into feelings of shame and a belief that I was unworthy. It was commonplace for me to feel inferior to others even when it was not warranted. I took control of this default thinking pattern when I realized that I no longer had to agree with it. I learned to filter out the voice of the disempowering inner critic who says that, "I am not good enough," and tune into the voice of the encouraging inner nurturer who says that "Who I am is enough," and "Making mistakes doesn't mean I am a failure." Our past shapes us, but it doesn't define who we are or what we can become.

What are the lies and negative beliefs buried inside that still impact you? I encourage you to identify the familiar nagging voices and exercise positive self-talk to motivate and empower yourself. Be kind and compassionate with yourself.

For me, the investment in myself through counseling and doing the inner work of self-examination greatly improved my-self-awareness and confidence. My journey and my faith fostered the healing process of my mental, emotional, and spiritual well-being. I gained a profound understanding that I am loved, and I found my worth and value in a powerful and loving God. A sense of hope, joy, confidence, and freedom lifted and displaced the heaviness in my heart.

Embrace Yourself

As I searched for and discovered who I was at the core, I peeled off some internalized labels and disposed of unhealthy beliefs. Not to mention, I rewired my thinking gradually, and learned to accept some of the positive feedback that I had previously brushed off.

We all need others to highlight our talents and point out our blind spots when it comes to our strengths and weaknesses. It was my sister who reminded me that my interpersonal strength was evident in my youth, when strangers would approach me by chance for directions (however, my sense of direction often resulted in mis-guidance), or start lengthy conversations on the bus or plane rides. I never thought much of these random encounters, but I now under-stand that I had a unique quality that led total strangers to willingly share their stories with me. My warm personality, humor, and atten-tiveness allowed me to make meaningful connections with people, no matter their background. My family and close friends validated my other strengths, telling me I am empathetic, witty, curious, and genuine. These affirmations supported my previous desire to go into social work, which best aligned with my personality, gifts, and pas-sion. I have since returned to school and switched my career path. I now work harder and live with more conviction than I ever have.

Whether it is a partner, a friend, or a mentor, I have realized that we need to surround ourselves with individuals who accept us for who we are. It's essential to be grounded in a firm foundation, be it spirituality or healthy connections, so that tides of life won't drag us down. I am thankful to have a support system that affirms me, and a husband who believes in me time and again when I lose sight of myself. It's never too late to build a sound support system for yourself, for you are worthy of love and respect.

The job loss was a catalyst of change in my life that resulted in a much needed reset in my adult years. Being let go was challenging and also a blessing in many ways: It forced me to take a hard look at myself, peel back the layers, and discover who I really was. Engineering was my layover spot prior to entering the field of social work; a career that gives me joy and purpose. There are lessons learned and takeaways from every obstacle in our lives. The key is to learn to develop a growth mindset so that we lighten our luggage and embrace the next adventure in our life's journey with open minds. I am continually learning to distinguish the negative voices and replace them with positive self-talk, all the while being mindful of my own thoughts and feelings and practicing self-validation. My hope is that you too, will take flight and discover your unique strengths and recognize that you are inherently worthy. Let's stay true to ourselves and live our lives confidently and unapologetically.

Chapter 10
Nature's Path to Confidence

Karen S. Richter

"We all have gifts. It's just a question of whether we access them, and feel confident enough to share them. Allow nature to show you how easy and enjoyable the path to finding your creative, confident self can be!"

After twenty years in the corporate HR space and twelve years as a business owner, Karen is finally (joyfully!) living life authentically and to the fullest. Her journey from self-doubt and exhaustion to confidence and fulfillment has uncovered many truths that she eagerly shares with others.

Karen has had a very accomplished career as a certified coach, facilitator, and leadership development consultant. She believed her success was the result of "powering through" her feelings of insecurity, inadequacy, and even invisibility. She fought against her natural introverted tendencies, feeling like she had to act like someone else in order to be heard and taken seriously. However, the resulting feelings of inauthenticity and "imposter syndrome" kept her exhausted, unsatisfied, and separated from all the richness life had to offer. She began to shed the "costume" of the professional, corporate image she thought was expected of her, and gave herself permission to allow the adventurous, nature-loving Karen to be seen by others. This resulted in more confidence, ease, and abundance.

Karen is the founder of www.CohesiveOutcomes.com and is thrilled to share her discoveries with female entrepreneurs who struggle with feelings of insecurity and unworthiness, helping them discover authentic confidence.

www.CohesiveOutcomes.com

ig: CohesiveOutcomes ~ fb: CohesiveOutcomes

li: Karen S. Richter ~ YouTube: CohesiveOutcomes

Could it really be that easy? Had I really found a quick, easy, and *fun* solution to the issue? An issue with which I didn't even realize I was challenged?

The issue started as a gentle nagging—a knowing that I didn't want to acknowledge, so I continued to push it deeper into the recesses of my mind. But the truth was, I was missing out on my life. I was a bystander, a zombie, sleepwalking through life. I was bogged down in the mundane routine, simply going through the motions.

To feel better about myself, I found much of my self-worth in my ability to solve problems, being the "fixer." I focused on everyone else, viewing the sacrifice of my own needs and wants as honorable. I lacked confidence and held myself back, seeking the comfort of the safety net I had knit for myself.

The period of my life when I felt most alive was as a mom to my babies. But those toddlers turned into young adults and started leaving home . . . What was my purpose now? What impact had I made on the world?

I wanted more out of life—I wanted to feel like I was truly a part of it. And that I made a difference.

As I tried to be satisfied with my ordinary life, some questions began to haunt me: Was it possible that it wasn't just me that was missing out, but everyone who interacted with me was missing out because I was only bringing part of myself to the situation? Was it conceivable that I actually had gifts to share and that I was depriving the world of those gifts by keeping them hidden below the surface? These questions caused me to feel guilty and examine the situation a little more deeply.

I've always considered myself to be a fairly happy person with a wonderful life. I learned from an early age that it was best to persevere. Don't dwell on the adversity, keep your chin up, look for the positive. Sounds like a good plan, right? This taught me to be positive and recognize that I had it much better than most others, so it made sense for me to help others. It also caused me to want to display the perfection in my life, to always BE PERFECT! In an effort to be perfect, I did well in school, stayed out of trouble (mostly . . . but those are stories for another day), advanced quickly in my career, and did all the expected "mom" things.

And yet, striving to be perfect was preventing me from experiencing life to the fullest.

It became clear to me that I couldn't be perfect in everyone's eyes because everyone had a different definition of perfect. It was unreasonable to think I could meet everyone's expectations —I'd always be letting someone down, which led to constant suffering. But I kept trying. I had to find ways to be even better. I put all my focus on other people and their needs and desires. I lost track of who I truly was inside. Decisions were made based not on what I wanted or what would make me happy, but on what would help me maintain that illusion of perfection. Being perfect would keep me safe and people would like me, or at least approve of me.

I was hiding my true self in an attempt to provide the world with the perfect me.

I tried not to focus on the exhaustion and suffering this created because I didn't want to be seen as whiny when, in the overall scheme of things, I had so much to be thankful for. I didn't feel like I could complain because I hadn't suffered any significant injustice, health disaster, or trauma, so I didn't feel I needed "healing." But that was just another "I'm not worthy" falsehood—I've had my fair share of adversity, but I didn't allow myself to see it as such because I could always compare myself to someone else and my struggles didn't match up with theirs.

There were things I started but didn't finish, for fear of "putting myself out there" and being less than perfect. As part of my coaching business, I created an amazing nature walk for women wanting to learn more about themselves and to create calm amid chaos. I found the perfect trail in a nearby state park with great places alongside the babbling brook in the woods where we could stop and reflect and write in our journals. It also had a steeper, more challenging hike on the cliffs on the opposite side of the creek where we could push ourselves beyond our perceived limits. It was going to be absolutely wonderful!

I never marketed it. I was afraid it wouldn't be perfect—I was afraid *I* wouldn't be perfect. ·

I now realize there are women who would've benefited significantly from this guided retreat through the woods. These women would have thought this retreat was the perfect solution, providing them with an escape from the daily grind and an opportunity to connect with themselves to determine what they really wanted to put their focus and energy on.

They didn't get it. Because I was too afraid to put it (and myself) out there.

I also think about the wasted hours I've spent avoiding these uncomfortable feelings. Instead of doing things that would allow me to grow and expand, I've numbed the pain with social media and games on my phone. (But they're "good games," helping to develop my brain, so they are okay, right?!)

What would my life (and the lives of those around me) look like if I could be an active participant instead of just an observer? A bystander?

I realized the possibilities were endless—and oh, so exciting! But how could I make that change?

Then came an amazing revelation that changed everything.

I loved being out in nature ever since I was a small child. I appreciated her beauty and felt so peaceful and capable while enjoying a walk in the woods, or a kayak on a still lake on a summer evening. But I didn't realize the healing, and the confidence, that comes from spending time in nature.

One particularly enjoyable nature activity for me is swimming. I have had the great fortune of going snorkeling over colorful coral reefs, which made an already awesome activity even better. Snorkeling transported me to a different world. A world of beauty, peace, and calmness.

On our honeymoon, my husband and I planned to get our scuba diving certification on the reefs off Belize. It excited me to learn something new but I didn't really think scuba diving could be any better than snorkeling. Snorkeling was so lovely—how could anything top it?

The undersea world enveloped me as I dove deep into water, becoming one with the environment. The edge of where my body ended and the water began was infinite. I had never felt so welcomed, as if I truly belonged with the school of brilliant blue and yellow fish that swam around me. No longer an outsider gazing into the water from the surface, I was completely immersed into my surroundings. I still can't find the words to adequately describe how loved that made me feel, and how supported and powerful.

I realized that experience explained my entire life perfectly.

I had been satisfied with the truly wonderful life I was living; I was content to sit back and watch life happen around me, happen *to* me. Just like I loved snorkeling and couldn't fathom that anything could be better than that. I was satisfied to skim the surface, unaware there could be more brilliance and life that would leave me feeling powerful and in awe of the universe. It took scuba diving to open my eyes to the abundance available to me.

American author Starhawk talks about her "transformation from a tourist in nature to an inhabitant,"[1] which so eloquently describes my own transition from observer to participant.

What are the benefits of becoming this inhabitant? Life overflows with more richness due to the confidence that comes from belonging, especially to something so much bigger than myself.

We've heard for years that being in nature makes us happier, healthier, and less stressed. Regular immersion in nature has health benefits such as reduced blood pressure, anxiety, stress levels, and risk of cancer, all while boosting immunity. Emotional benefits of spending time in nature have been shown to include being happier, more empathetic, more compassionate, and bringing greater meaning to relationships.

The benefits of nature go beyond physical and psychological health. Recent cognitive studies have shown that being in nature improves cognitive ability and creativity. A team from Stanford

---

1   Starhawk. *The Earth Path: Grounding Your Spirit in the Rhythms of Nature*. New York, New York: HarperSanFrancisco, 2004, 5.

University found that taking a fifty-minute walk in nature resulted in an increase in "working memory performance," as well as "decreased anxiety, rumination, and negative affect, and preservation of positive affect."[2] This study's conclusion was not based on self-reported feelings, but on actual measurements of activity in the brain in various areas responsible for different functions. The area of our brains that is activated by brooding (focusing on negative aspects of our lives, which can lead to anxiety and depression) showed lessened activity after a nature walk.

Similarly, students in Scandinavian countries spend more time outdoors and consistently perform at the top end of the academic scale globally.

"Nature acts as a spiritual sanctuary that provides us with clarity during challenging times . . . Nature helps us get out of our heads and into our hearts."[3] This is a big one for me. I've often been told to "stop thinking so much" and to "get into my heart space." But how? Now I know, the answer is nature.

Nature allows us to become awestruck. When we are blinded by the beauty of a sunset, we are beyond a cognitive state and simply experience what is happening in the moment. We don't judge, label, or try to explain. We simply enjoy the moment. How zen, right? Being in this space of awe allows us to stop thinking, and that's when the ingenious solution to a problem "magically" pops into our head. When we allow our minds to rest and become still, we find we have more ah-ha moments. Just like when we "sleep on it," we allow our unconscious mind to work.

Observing nature reminds us that nature doesn't ruminate about what was, or what will be. It simply exists in the moment. We're advised to live in the moment, but we often find that hard to do. Seeing the stream change its course when an obstacle, such as a fallen tree, lays in its way, or seeing the gnarly trees that grow in the wind remind us that flexibility pays off. We are reminded that we

2   Gregory N. Bratman, Gretchen C. Daily, Benjamin J. Levy, and James J. Gross. "The benefits of nature experience: Improved affect and cognition." *Landscape and Urban Planning* 138, (June 2015): 41-50, https://doi.org/10.1016/j.landurbplan.2015.02.005

3   Andrés R. Edwards, *Renewal: How Nature Awakens Our Creativity, Compassion, and Joy* (Gabriola Island, British Columbia, Canada: New Society Publishers, 2019), chapter 1.

can prevail when we see the beautiful green leaves on the magnolia tree emerge even after a late frost turned all the beautiful pink flowers to crusty brown. Seeing something as simple as a tiny sapling growing out of a hole in a much larger tree, or pushing through cracks in the rocks (or did they cause the crack?) fills me with the belief that I can be strong and do mighty things.

It doesn't have to be a major activity to benefit from being in nature.

In 2015, the Human Spaces Report found that workers with greenery and sunlight in their environments have a fifteen percent higher level of well-being, a six percent higher level of productivity, and a fifteen percent higher level of creativity than people who work in spaces devoid of nature.[4] As an entrepreneur, I know I want to benefit from those statistics!

Here are some simple things you can do to experience the benefits of nature right away:

- Bring nature into your office. I have rearranged my office to face the windows and look out at the trees and creek passing by. I've incorporated a few live plants and am establishing the habit of bringing fresh-cut flowers into my office weekly.

- Dig your fingers and toes into the dirt. Exposure to bacteria in the soil can activate brain cells that improve mood, reduce anxiety, and enhance learning. Yet another significant benefit of gardening—not just the resulting healthy veggies or beautiful flowers, but the effect of the bacteria.

- Read outside. This doesn't take any additional time if you'd be reading anyway, right?

- Get outside and take a walk. Challenge yourself to thirty minutes in nature for thirty days.

---

4   *Human Spaces: The Global Impact of Biophilic Design in the Workplace* (Interface Inc., 2015) https://greenplantsforgreenbuildings.org/wp-content/uploads/2015/08/Human-Spaces-Report-Biophilic-Global_Impact_Biophilic_Design.pdf

- Be on the lookout for beauty in nature. Breathe in the glorious scenery around you. Be curious! Explore! Journal about it!

- Look for patterns in nature. Simple patterns (patterns wind creates on a field of tall grass, ripples along the creek, colorful flowers dotting the landscape) can set our creative minds free. We search for connections and often make associations we hadn't thought of before. I often find a potential solution that has been lurking in the back of my mind when I allow my brain to seek these patterns in nature.

- Immerse yourself in nature. I consciously work to go beyond simply observing what's around me, even if that observation includes appreciation (similar to an observer viewing a painting in an art gallery). Instead, I work to become one with the natural surroundings. What messages are the trees, animals, clouds, stars trying to convey to me? This awareness of my surroundings allows me to realize that I am just a small part of the scenery, and that takes the focus off me. I no longer feel like I'm in the spotlight, which is such a relief and gives me permission to relax into my authentic self.

- Turn to nature for guidance; allow it to be a mentor. Identifying the qualities in nature that we appreciate gives us insight into our own characters. Take cues from nature. Nature isn't trying to please everyone in every situation. Look at the flowers: Does the pink rose worry that it's not as bright as the red rose? Does the lone sunflower look any less brilliant than the group of sunflowers in the field?

It's not always easy to make nature a priority. We make changes, but then life gets in the way and we fall back into old habits. Sometimes I feel like I'm too busy to fit in a "frivolous" walk. That's where a simple perspective shift can help. Don't look at these activities as frivolous—acknowledge that they are part of a healthy routine. Recognize that you will be better able to serve the world by taking a few minutes to rejuvenate.

Keep yourself motivated by finding a friend or group that will be supportive and encouraging.

Whatever changes you decide to make, you'll have more success at sticking with them if you make them fun. Invite your inner child to play.

If you question whether you have a light to share with the world—*you do*. We all have gifts. It's just a question of whether we access them, and feel confident enough to share them.

Allow nature to show you how easy and enjoyable the path to finding your creative, confident self can be!

Chapter 11
A Second Chance at Life

Antonietta Botticelli

"You Do You."

In 2016, Antonieta was diagnosed as a full-blown diabetic, could not tie her shoes, walk more than twenty minutes, and had a twenty percent chance of dying. Fast forward to June 2018: she lost 141 pounds, kicked diabetes to the curb, became a certified group fitness instructor, created a fitness program called abotti, and reduced her chances of dying to less than five percent.

She developed an infectious and engaging community across the country, wherein she inspires and motivates others to live their best and healthiest lives.

abotti with Antonietta is a fun, low-impact group fitness experience that incorporates everyday practical movements. Everyone is welcomed—all ages, all fitness levels, all genders—it is essentially a party with real people, like you and me.

www.abotti.ca

ig: abottiwithantonietta ~ fb: abottiwithantonietta

I died. Here is my story of how I came back to life.

I reflect on my childhood; the time leading up to my death, and I feel that growing up in an Italian household was the greatest thing; I was always surrounded by a huge family and a circle of friends. At all times, there was an abundance of laughter, fun, and food. I never felt alone. Loyalty, respect, and generosity fueled my blood, my mind, and my soul. Family and friends came first.

My childhood was great. My parents loved us kids, took care of us, and made us feel safe. We did fun things together as a family all the time. We were not spoiled with material things, but instead my parent's top priority was to always support and comfort us. We lived a very simple life.

My father is the reason I am the woman I am today. He always told me I was the greatest thing: smart, kind, and simply amazing. He would introduce me to others that way. My self-confidence, fearless attitude, and strong work ethic came from my father's strong belief in me—in what I could do and how I would impact the world.

High school was the best time of my life. I belonged to many different circles of friends, was involved with a variety of school programs, and did very well academically. I was a happy, confident, and social young woman. Life was *great*!

I dated a boy in my last year of high school who was sweet, kind, and said things to me that made me feel adored, loved, and special. He swept me off my feet with his charm and romance. I was in love. Then, as time went by, our relationship slowly shifted in an unhealthy way.

Here is where I died. The Antonietta I had known was no more.

The relationship was not always awful, but it had more bad than good. It was toxic, and I didn't even realize it. It slowly killed my self-confidence, my desire to do fun things, my excitement and joy in life. I became a completely different person, altering my bright and fun personality, my morals and beliefs, and even the way I physically looked and my dreams for who I wanted to become.

He had a subtle way of making me believe I ate too much, did not work as hard as he did, did not look as good as he did, was not good enough for him, was not pretty enough, not worthy enough. It was too much for me to handle.

The relationship changed the person I'd been before I met him. I was so unhappy that I lost myself. I lost my voice, my spunk, my passion for life, and my smile. My mental, emotional, and physical state was negatively affected by his manipulative behavior. I started to shut down. I did not want to go on holidays or go out with friends. I hid inside my house and turned to food for comfort. I gained 160 pounds and I was too embarrassed to see friends or family who I had not seen in many years. I know, what a mess!

I resented him. How could he treat me this way, and how did I allow it? How did I go from Ms. Confident and Full of Life to a woman who no longer gave a shit about anything, and avoided the beautiful things that life offered? I hated myself for allowing that to happen. I was angry, hurt, and disappointed.

The day came when I mustered up the courage to say *yes* to ending the relationship. It was one of the hardest things I've done, but I did not realize at the time that it was the *greatest* moment of my life. It was difficult to move on, but I took a deep breath and did what needed to be done. I cried a lot during that time. The separation, finding a new place to live, and coming to terms with the fact that my relationship was over was new and confusing to me.

My new chapter allowed me the opportunity to live life differently. I finally did what I wanted to do, the way I wanted to do it. I was no longer being controlled. I could finally make my own choices and do things I wanted to do. I moved into a different style home, bought a car model that wouldn't have been approved of in my old life, and decorated my home to look the way I wanted. My new life was not all bells and whistles, and it was definitely not easy at first. I had a lot of work to do to get *me* back.

During this time, I was so unhealthy that I ended up in the hospital with Type 2 Diabetes; I'd come very close to slipping into a diabetic coma. I had trouble tying my shoes. It was a struggle for me to walk, even for twenty minutes. All I did was work nonstop—full time at my corporate job—come home, eat, and sleep. The next day, I did the same thing. It was a very robotic lifestyle. I didn't want to do anything adventurous because I couldn't physically and didn't want to emotionally. I wanted to stay home and avoid what was out in the world.

Here is where I came back to life.

In September of 2016, I began to get Antonietta back. It started with me getting healthy and working on my journey to wellness. I joined a weight-loss program. Man, was that hard and scary. I felt completely uncomfortable and vulnerable. Every ounce of me did not want to face the music of how bad my health had gotten. It was easier to tuck it under the rug and just keep my blinders on. Little did I know that walking through those doors would be the beginning of a new, exciting, and great adventure. What followed is an incredible story that is still being played out today, and I still can't believe it's my life.

Realizing that I fought to recreate my life is its own victory. Making a mindful decision to take care of and work on yourself is one of the toughest and most important things you can do. Identifying the joys in your life and focusing on what matters to you is the key to living a full and happy life. Joy comes in many forms and being present in your everyday life gives you the courage and strength to continue forward. You are your biggest cheerleader.

So, how did Antonietta get herself back? How did she manage to dig herself out of a very dark hole? How did she get a second chance at life?

Simple. She came to understand her worth. Her worthiness to be happy, to be healthy, to accept the love, kindness, and generosity of others. To fully accept and understand that she is worth the successes that came her way. She worked hard. She played hard. She loved hard. She prayed hard.

I knew I had to change my weight to give me the jump start I needed to feel better about myself. I hid for too long, and had already lost so much precious time. Choosing to lose weight gave me permission to enjoy life and the people surrounding me.

For the first time in a long time, my mindset, determination, and focus all came together. How did that happen? What did I do to get there mentally?

Thank goodness for friends. They were the light at the end of a dark tunnel. When I close my eyes and think of all the people who helped me, I get emotional. What did I do to deserve these beautiful people in my life? Let me give you a glimpse of what these people did; Their acts of kindness saved my life: Laurie, who texted me every day—and I mean every single day—for three years to ask me what my sugar levels were. She checked up on me to make sure I was okay. Just thinking about her and what she did gets me all choked up. She is an incredible human. Lesley, who asked me to walk with her every morning for twenty minutes, played a huge role in my journey to wellness. The first time she asked me was in 2016 and we still walk together to this day. Shannon, who asked me to join a weight-loss program with her, impacted me in a *big* way. Vee, who has supported me since day one. Her love and encouragement helped me to jump at any and every opportunity. She was and still is my security blanket. These are a few of the people who played an integral role at the beginning of my wellness journey. Others followed them, and I received help and encouragement from many. Thinking about their kindness sends chills down my spine. I will be forever grateful to them. There are too many to mention.

The first thing I needed to understand was that to make significant changes, I needed to visually see a change. It would motivate me to keep going. Weight loss was my number one priority, and I visually saw a number on a scale change every week. I made realistic weekly goals and I achieved them. I knew I needed that to keep me motivated and focused.

My journey to wellness hit a roadblock one morning at weigh-in. I lost my targeted amount of weight every week until I hit a total weight loss of 58.6 pounds. The next week's goal was to lose 1.4 pounds to reach a total weight loss of sixty pounds. That was all I focused on that week. Yet, the scale did not budge. For the very first time, I did not hit my goal. I was devastated, upset, and shocked, to say the very least. I left and quit the weight loss program. I actually quit—I was done. I couldn't believe I did not hit my goal weight for the week. I was deflated. The scale ruled my life.

I ran out of the building, got into my truck, and took off. I felt defeated. I ended up pulling into a parking lot where I bawled my eyes out. I convinced myself that I was not good enough. Then my phone rang. My dear friend Lesley told me to pull up my socks, get back at it, and reminded me that I was a champ. That moment was pivotal in my wellness journey. If I had given up on myself that day, I wouldn't have lost another eighty pounds. Sometimes, you need a friendly reminder of how far you have come, encouragement to keep going and to never give up on yourself.

In May 2018, my friend Paula and I went on a cruise that was hosted by the weight-loss program we were members of. We were super excited to meet the team behind the scenes and others who were on the same wellness journey as we were. One of these people was a phenomenal woman named Sue. She was part of the crew who helped greet members on the ship and was the fitness instructor of a low-impact cardio class offered to us.

Sue's fitness class was called *Walk 15 with Sue*. At that time, both Paula and I thought it meant that we would walk with her for fifteen minutes around the ship. Well, that was not the case at all. When we shared this with Sue, she burst into laughter. She took our hands, brought us on stage, and told us to get ready to be blown away.

Getting up on that stage with Sue and Paula literally changed my life. When I looked out into the crowd, I was overcome with emotion. Everyone was taking part. It did not matter your size, age, or fitness level. Everyone was enjoying themselves and moving. Sue was a firecracker. She played upbeat music, made the workout *fun,* and you left feeling so great about yourself. I realized at that moment that I wanted to do this—I wanted to bring this to my hometown and was determined to become a *Walk 15* instructor.

In July of 2018, I launched in Stouffville. I had no idea what to expect, or if there would be any actual interest. My plan was to offer the class once a week for six weeks. Imagine how shocked I was when sixty-seven people showed up on the first night. The program grew from once a week, to twice a week, and then three times a week. The word spread to other surrounding areas and I opened up classes in Aurora, Uxbridge, and Vaughan.

Fall of 2019, I decided to venture out on my own and resigned from my corporate job. I created my very own program called abotti, a low-impact group fitness experience incorporating everyday practical movements. I am extremely proud to say that I created a movement known as You Do You, and offer a fitness environment that is judgment-free and inclusive to everyone.

I launched abotti in January of 2020, and then COVID-19 hit in March. In-person classes came to a screeching halt, but the community desperately needed to stay together and remain connected. I instantaneously offered complimentary abotti classes via Zoom in the living room of my friends, Catherine and Emily, which then moved to their basement, known as the "abotti studio." I have since moved out of their basement and have my very own abotti studio in Stouffville. I am very grateful to them for all they have done.

When I reflect, my life has not been easy. It has had its moments of struggles, heartaches, and disappointments, but it has also had its share of excitement, laughter, love, and fun. Every day, I choose to live my very best life possible and continue the work on my own personal development. I give daily gratitude to God for always being there for me and I wake up every morning excited to take on the day.

My life experiences have taught me many lessons. I have learned to never give up on myself, even when life gets tough. Yes, it may be easier to give up, but tough times are not meant to destroy me, they are meant for me to step into my power. Saying yes to things that are out of my comfort zone empowers me to do hard things. Surrounding myself with like-minded, encouraging, and supportive people allows me to keep going, to always be true to myself, and to finally understand that self-care is not selfish, and that I am worth it.

Chapter 12
Finding the Strength

Amy P. K. Wong

"Having the opportunity to share my story through writing and being able to make heartfelt connections with others is how I have been able to find the strength to embrace, to grieve, and to cope. I don't believe I will heal 100% and I am at peace with that. I know that I am heading towards a happier tomorrow. Baby steps."

Amy P. K. Wong is a proud, loving mother of two young boys, a happy wife of nineteen years this August, a family photographer, and a good food ambassador with Epicure. During the first eighteen months of the COVID-19 pandemic, Amy took on the role as a teacher when she and her husband, John, agreed it was best to homeschool their boys. That's when Amy rediscovered her love of writing. Looking through the boys' homework, it brought back many happy memories of composition writing in elementary school and poetry writing in highschool. When Amy was approached with a chance to contribute to this book, it was a dream come true! The timing couldn't have been more perfect. Now, she can add co-author to her resume!

amywong.epicure.com/en-ca/

ig: amyshomecooking ~ fb: amyshomecooking, AmyWong

li: amy-wong-395b74169

L et's go back to fifteen years ago. John and I had been married for four years. Growing up, my expectations for my life were quite simple: go to school, find a job, fall in love, get married, and start a family. Simple, yet happy! By the time John and I got married, we were actually considering not having any children at all. We were enjoying our married life—sleeping in on the weekends, eating when we were hungry, watching movies with cinematic surround sound blasting, staying up as late as we wanted, taking road trips just because it was sunny out . . . . We were free as birds! In addition, we have plenty of nephews and nieces to spoil.

One day, it happened. Everything was different. Our friends were getting pregnant and having babies. I had thought we could live without babies of our own; my heart told me otherwise. From the first look at our friends' precious baby, to the fresh smell of the baby's scent, to the soft touch of the baby's tiny fingers, John and I knew we had to follow our hearts. We wanted a baby together.

Let the fun begin! We tried for three months and I got pregnant! I didn't have any morning sickness. I was energetic. I had a great appetite. Life was good. As soon as our pregnancy hit the twelve week mark, we made the announcement to our families and our closest friends. Everyone was ecstatic for us!

After a wonderful weekend, it was business as usual and we both went back to work. I remember it was a beautiful Monday, so sunny and warm. I even went for a walk with my co-worker during our lunch break to soak in the sun and get some exercise for the little one. Everything felt great. I felt great! Little did I know, all that was about to change . . .

There were thirty minutes left of work and, as usual, I needed a washroom break. That's when I noticed something was wrong—I was spotting. I was not in pain, but there was blood. I started to panic. I frantically called one of my best friends to ask her what I should do. She suggested I call my obstetrician or go straight to the ER. I called my obstetrician's office and the receptionist told me to head straight to the ER to get a full examination.

When John and I arrived at the ER, the waiting area seemed extremely busy. The air felt stuffy and stale. I was starting to feel nauseous. Since I was still bleeding, they attended to me almost immediately and I was sent straight to ultrasound. When I returned, John and I were silent as we anxiously waited. Our hands locked tight together, as if we were praying as one.

The ER was still swarming with patients and the doctors and nurses seemed to be running in circles. I was feeling nauseous again and couldn't breathe. Then I heard my name. I froze. I couldn't answer. I felt like I had lost my voice. John answered the doctor on my behalf. The doctor looked at me sympathetically. My heart sank deeper and deeper, as he told us the technician couldn't find a heartbeat or any movement in my ultrasound. I cried uncontrollably and before I knew it, I began hyperventilating. Nurses came rushing over. They told me to slow down my breathing but I couldn't. I felt like something had taken over my body and I was no longer in control. *Where's John?* I realized I was no longer holding John's hand because I was surrounded by so many doctors and nurses. I felt more lost than ever. I felt more alone than ever.

How was John feeling? Was he okay? Was anyone taking care of him? The baby was not just my loss; the baby was our loss. He must have been devastated, too.

When I finally calmed down, I felt the entire room fall silent and all eyes were on me. I felt embarrassed, beyond devastated, and incredibly lost. I wanted to curl into a ball and hide in a corner. The one thing that kept me sane was knowing John was with me. I was not alone. I was once again safe in his warm embrace. I felt his sadness, but I also felt his strength. He was physically supporting my frail body but, most importantly, supporting my broken heart. Supporting *both* our broken hearts.

The last time I cried this hard was when my grandmother passed. Her death was sudden and unexpected. I didn't get to have a proper goodbye. I felt the very same sadness here; I didn't get to say goodbye. When I lost my grandmother, I felt darkness for six long months. I was afraid of what the future held for me and John after we lost our child. I didn't want the same darkness to take over.

The next few phone calls were the hardest ones we ever had to make. We had just announced our pregnancy over the weekend, and now we had to tell everyone the baby was gone. I struggled profusely in making the calls. I couldn't even get the words out. John had to muster up the strength to finish the conversations that I couldn't even start. I sobbed on his chest as he made each call. I felt the pain in his beating heart. I felt the sadness in his gentle voice. I felt the weight of his pain, as each call became harder and harder for him to make.

A million questions started rushing through my head. Was this miscarriage my fault? Did I consume the wrong foods or drinks? Should I have stayed at my desk during my lunch breaks? Was I wearing the wrong shoes? Were my clothes too tight or too loose? Did I strain myself without realizing it? Did I get out of bed the wrong way? What could I have done to prevent this from happening? Why did my baby leave so soon? Were we not meant to be parents? Was I not meant to be a mother?

I had so many questions. Yet, I had no answers.

Even though we knew our baby was no longer with us, the next twenty-four hours made everything more real, more raw, and even more heartbreaking. There was a final step to completing this nightmare. I had to take medication to help my cervix dilate and to have my uterine lining shed. It would feel like a full-on labor, with all the bleeding, cramps and pain . . . but without the joy of having a baby. If I didn't take the medication, I would risk an infection and/or incomplete miscarriage, which could cause a dilation and curettage surgery at a later date. I had to let go.

The following days were extremely somber. Mentally, I was a wreck. We were filled with sadness and regret. Should we have tried having a baby much earlier in our marriage? Did we wait too long? Why didn't we deserve this baby? My head was filled with so many questions, and yet again, with no answers.

The following week, we saw my obstetrician. She said the medication worked well and my body would heal itself in the coming months. She wanted us to know that miscarriages, unfortunately, were very common, especially with the first pregnancy. We could try again in six months, after my body had time to heal.

We were both hesitant to say what was on our minds, but it was something we needed to discuss. Did we want to try for another baby? This experience literally crushed our hearts and souls. What if we try, become pregnant, and have another miscarriage? Even if my body could have handled another loss, I don't know if my mind could. We were so conflicted. Then we realized we were only this conflicted because we both genuinely wanted to have a baby together. As tough as the road ahead of us may be, we decided to try again in six months.

The next few months went by quickly and quietly. We were starting to feel "normal" again. We learned to smile, laugh, and found the joy in life—even booking a much needed vacation. We used the time to allow our hearts to mend. We were ready.

At the six-months mark, we tried again and it happened! We got pregnant! I was pregnant! Was I happy? Extremely! Was I scared? Petrified! In fact, I was more scared than I was happy. But I knew I had to shake off all the negativity and flow with the excitement. This was our time to celebrate, stay positive, relax, and soak it all in. The baby will feel all the good vibes and become strong and healthy.

Did I have an easy second pregnancy? Not at all. I was on bed rest for almost seven out of the nine months, with many hospital visits. It was not an easy battle, but one worth fighting for. In the end, we won! John and I had a healthy baby boy at full term. It was surreal—I was a bit emotionless for the first few hours after labor. I felt a lot of guilt. I was holding this beautiful healthy boy in my arms, but all I could think of was, he could have had an older brother or sister. My heart was broken. I knew I should be celebrating but my mind wasn't in the right place.

I wanted to accept and cherish the moment with my newborn. I took a deep breath as I shed a few tears and started over. I looked down at this precious little human being, held his tiny fingers, and I fell in love. It took me a few hours, but once I got there, my love for him has never stopped, only grown. I didn't know it was possible to love someone so much. I am so grateful that Nathan chose me to be his mother.

John and I decided to have one more child, so Nathan would have a sibling. We knew there would be risks. I could be on bed rest again, I may have another miscarriage, or I may not even be able to get pregnant. We didn't know what would happen, but we knew we wanted to try for Nathan's sake. So we tried. This third pregnancy happened instantly! No time to wait or to plan. What a blessing. But as fate would have it, it was another incredibly hard pregnancy. I was on bed rest most of the time and, to make things more complicated, we were in a horrible car accident when I was six months pregnant.

It was a beautiful, sunny morning. We wanted to run some errands and I wanted to get some fresh air. Then, out of nowhere, an oncoming car headed straight into us! It hit us so hard that our car swerved towards a huge tree at the corner of the street. Thank goodness, John was able to hit the brakes in time. We were only a couple meters away from that thick solid tree trunk! I immediately jumped out of the car to see if Nathan was safe and unharmed. John and I both hugged Nathan tightly and kept asking him if he was okay. Nathan looked stunned but didn't look hurt. He was only eighteen months, and didn't understand what we were screaming and crying about.

Then John asked me if I was okay. I said, "I'm fine." He asked me again, worriedly. Then it dawned on me—I had forgotten I was pregnant! *Is our baby okay? Am I bleeding? Is the baby hurt?*

Immediately, I was rushed to the hospital. The paramedics, nurses, and doctors couldn't find the baby's heartbeat. Of course, my hyperventilating didn't help. I couldn't believe it was all happening again. I felt the world crumbling down on me. I was also scared of how Nathan was. He didn't know how to talk yet. Was he injured? Was he traumatized? How's John? Was he okay? He must be so terrified, not knowing how the baby and I were doing. I had to stay strong for the baby, Nathan, and John. I kept telling myself that the baby was okay. *We're all going to be fine, and I need to slow my breathing down.* Finally, we heard the baby's heartbeat! I let out a big sigh of relief. *Baby is a fighter. We're all fighters. We've got this!*

The remaining three months were filled with hospital visits and lots of bed rest. Baby number two was also born at full term. Another healthy baby boy! John and I were beyond relieved and felt very blessed once again. This time, I did not miss a moment. I looked down at Nicholas, shed a happy tear, and fell in love instantly. At that very moment, I felt like the luckiest person on earth. I have two precious, healthy boys who I loved (and still love) unconditionally. I couldn't ask for more. John and I were complete. Our little family of four.

Perfect or imperfect, this is our life now and I wouldn't change it for the world. My heart still breaks when I hear about someone having a miscarriage. I still close my eyes for a moment of silence, when someone in a movie loses their baby. I think having these feelings only means I'm human. Little by little, I am finding the strength to embrace, to grieve, to cope and to heal. Baby steps.

***

The stats show that one out of eight women will have a miscarriage. Knowing this does not make me feel better, but it does make me realize that I'm not alone. You are not alone. We are all human. Nothing is perfect. No one is. This chapter was written for you, your friend, your family member, or anyone you know who has ever experienced a miscarriage. It's been fifteen years and I'm still trying to find a way to heal the loss of my unborn child. I now have two healthy boys who I love dearly. Unfortunately, that doesn't fill the hole in my heart for my previous loss. However, I am writing this chapter to help grieve and to cope with my broken heart and soul. I hope this chapter will resonate with you. May this help you find peace and comfort, knowing you are not alone.

Chapter 13
A Soul Makeover Journey

Sandra Didomenico

"Uncover your truth, your soul, so that you can peel away the layers
to become the person you are meant to be."

Sandra is a successful wellness advocate and confidence coach who is passionate about guiding busy women toward finding clarity and self-acceptance. Through unblocking exercises, Sandra helps women lead a vibrant lifestyle.

She currently resides in the country by a lake in Sutton, Ontario, which is her dream setting. She lives with her husband and two adult kids. Sandra has faced many battles and suffered in silence as a stay-at-home mother. She struggled for many days, which led her into a downward spiral, feeling inadequate and unconfident. She discovered the path of personal development after being in the direct sales industry for ten years. She decided to do the inner work necessary for change, work she now calls a Soul Makeover. This guided her to true self-confidence, clear decision-making, and self-acceptance, once and for all. Sandra is now a certified confidence coach and works to empower others through sharing her life experiences. Her goal is to inspire others to own their tomorrows, and live a life with purpose, every single day. Sandra also offers social media confidence coaching to show others how to stand out from the crowd and let their voice be heard. She guides entrepreneurs toward becoming prepared for live video content for all social media platforms.

She has a thriving interview series called *Spice It Up with Sandra,* where she is passionate about interviewing entrepreneurs and encouraging them to share their stories. She too, is a well-known speaker. Connect with Sandra for a free discovery call!

www.sandradido.ca

ig: journeywithsandradido ~ fb: Sandradido8

li: www.sandradido.ca

H ow did it take me forty years to connect the dots about what was holding me back? How did I go from lacking confidence to having an abundance of confidence?

My early twenties were my prime years, when I was successfully working in the fashion industry. I was so confident and full of life—nothing could stand in my way. Except for my feelings of unworthiness. I wanted to feel heard, but I wondered, *how could that even be possible?* My parents were loving, generous, and inspiring, yet I still felt empty within.

For a girl who had great fashion sense, and proudly wore pink tights and mini skirts to school everyday, I had been suppressing fear, doubt, uncertainty, and feelings of anger deep down for some time. I was pretty confident in my younger years. I made friends easily, had a great childhood, loving parents, and stability. However, the emotional toll of my brother's battle with epilepsy, and the fear of the unknown for him, became evident later in my life.

Furthermore, I battled with my weight all my life. As an emotional eater, my weight would go up and down, marking countless days of binge eating, even after losing eighty pounds. My mother would find empty ice cream containers under my bed! Oh Lord!

As a child, I was bullied and made fun of for my weight. I was constantly nagged about watching what I ate. I was ridiculed on many occasions by my peers at school because I was out of shape and not slim like the others. I always walked alongside my beautiful, slim cousin, with whom I shared a lot of time, and I always left feeling less worthy and less beautiful than she was, like I walked in her shadow. This created a long-time relationship with food and binge eating, which would fluctuate constantly, and altered my confidence, since I did not feel self-acceptance because of how I looked. I often criticized myself in the mirror. I felt uncomfortable in my clothing and wanted to rush home and eat junk food. My parents were very focused on my brother, who battled for fourteen years with a strong form of epilepsy. I faced a long period of stress. I was unsure of the situation that existed, and was fearful that something drastic would happen to him. We often rushed to the hospital in the middle of the night when he had large seizures. This was scary for me at such a young age. I was not aware of how to deal with these emotions at the time, so they continued to be suppressed.

This was the mindset I became familiar with. And these emotions remained with me until recently. In my late forties, I had a revelation, an Aha Moment where I uncovered my old belief systems. I finally connected the dots! I realized something needed to be done to remove these emotional triggers.

The Love and Family Story

In my mid-twenties, I met a sweet Italian boy, thanks to my dear friends, who set us up. We married and began building a family. My life was a blessing in so many ways and yet I was still struggling, still feeling there was a void in my life. As my children began school, I became more aware of other women who were accomplishing so much more than I was. I felt heavy, heavy guilt, and an emptiness. Being a stay-at-home mom was the beginning of a journey of feeling unworthy and inadequate for a few years. Staying at home with our kids was so rewarding, and a decision my husband and I made together. And yet it took its toll on my mental well-being. I would wake up and do my mom duties, then feel hopeless for the rest of the day. I began feeling resentful and frustrated, and I took it out on my family at times. I knew deep down that something had to be done, however, I felt lost and kept this to myself for a long time.

You could say I faced impostor syndrome. I was trying to keep it together like the perfect, superwoman mother, and yet I was suffering in silence. I did not allow anyone to see what was really happening. I sought medical help, and for a short time, Prozac helped me find some light. It was a defining moment, and I felt shame. However, overall I began to see the light of happiness again, and of possibilities.

As I gained awareness over the years, it reminded me to immerse myself in personal growth. When I was introduced to the world of Direct Sales, it opened up my eyes to a new light, a new direction that included personal development and facing fears. This was an incredible journey that led me to my current role as a confidence coach.

At a meeting for my DS business, a woman who was a life coach was there demonstrating how everything is energy and what you think about, you bring about. I had never heard of a life coach. I know, you're wondering: Where have I been? Looking back, I had obviously tuned out the world for a while.

I listened to her and it was as if she was speaking right to me—like I was the only one in the room! It was a defining moment in my life, a spark of hope that I had not felt for ages. I had goosebumps. I had butterflies. I had many emotions come through me that evening. I was compelled to seek guidance from this woman. I worked with her, and it was by far the best decision and investment I made for myself. I began a journey where I could get very clear on what I wanted for myself and for who I was meant to become. I had decided this was going to be the year of *me!*

Blindsided By Fears

Let's take a few moments to go back in history. Let's look at the moments when I found myself in vulnerable relationships and business partnerships. These were times when I sabotaged my self-worth. I was a people pleaser. I often went out of my way to please others rather than myself even if it was inconvenient . I would allow others to overpower me, in conversations, in my daily share of the products and services I offered. It was a repeated pattern that I finally noticed in my late forties. I was being taken advantage of over and over, blindsided by the fears of standing tall on my own. I had this inner fear of handling my business completely solo. I felt the urge to always lean on others who were overbearing, with stronger personalities than myself. I was simply not confident. How did this happen? Why was I attracting this into my life?

It deeply hurt me on many occasions. This brought me down, and I felt unworthy and incapable. I knew I had to shift old belief patterns *now* and free myself of any obligations to anyone other than myself. I had to seek and find self love for myself again.

These were the life lessons I was destined to go through. I had to hit my own rock bottom and experience the defining moments that made me who I am today. I struggled with being loyal to others. I could not understand why other people would intentionally hurt me. I was frustrated, angry with myself for allowing this to happen. This was a tough period. However, it's also when I decided to use these lessons to propel myself into becoming more confident. And that is exactly what I did!

Soul Makeover

It was time to reset my belief systems and find my worthiness and self-acceptance, once and for all. I learned to surrender to everything; *surrender* became my new found word—it was so freeing!

My battles with my weight, my battles with worthiness, my battles with perfection, my battles with loneliness. I figured I deserved a fulfilled successful life, too. I now live consciously every moment of every day.

The hard lessons had to do with the toxic relationships and negative people I was keeping in my life. I had to learn that I was the one who kept them there, because I was too caring and giving. That was my nature. I ended up in these situations because I had fears of leaning on myself solely; I didn't feel strong enough to do so. This came from my past beliefs about standing on my own, as my brother was not always well enough to be present in my life. I came to these realizations through timeline therapy, for which I am forever grateful. I also had to learn to set boundaries, which was a new word I had to embrace.

Now, I am just a badass woman! I have developed a thicker skin and pleasing people is not part of my life any longer.

I uncovered the *light. I decided* that enough was enough and that I would stand tall and reinvent myself. Can one reinvent themselves? Absolutely! I am living proof of it.

I decided I would follow the passions I was destined to follow. I would put myself out there, even if it felt scary, to see the kinds of results that fueled my confidence more and more.

How did I do that? I read a lot of books! I attended DS conferences; I empowered myself through countless affirmations and

YouTube videos, every single day, by the world's top motivators. I tuned into my subconscious mind and I amplified my resources. It was about embracing the inner work, and it definitely paid off!

Today, I guide other women to get very clear on their own worthiness and self-acceptance so they can move into the life they deserve and design. Sometimes, facing the truth is hard—I certainly understand that! And there are many times we must go through the experiences, good or bad, to get to where we are meant to be. I am grateful for all that I went through as it allowed me the path I am on today, as a stronger woman mentally and emotionally. I have made the connection of mind, body, and soul that surpasses all emotions to a level of opulence and light. This is what I call a Soul Makeover: a journey where one unravels their old belief systems and embraces self-acceptance, finding clarity in their soul's purpose.

I began this journey of self-discovery and, truthfully, I will never finish that journey. It is ever-evolving, and it's one's life experiences that guide us on the path.

However, we are also the driving force of our destination. Wouldn't you say so?

The following tools are the tools that guided me to the greatness of who I am. Want to reinvent yourself? Here is your guide.

Self-Love

The power of love and loving yourself is profound. You may ask, *How does one get to this point of complete self-love?* It takes a lot of inner work and being comfortable with who you are right now. It means having self-acceptance and finding peace of mind that you are doing your best. You are beautiful, inside and out. I recommend reflecting on yourself, meditating and zoning in on your body. Appreciate each part of your body. From head to toe. It is an incredible experience!

Affirmations

The power of repeating affirming statements is life-changing. This has impacted my mindset in such a positive manner and boosted my confidence. Our subconscious mind is a sponge and we can implement new emotions and affirming words to empower us daily.

There is scientific evidence that affirmations activate the reward center's prefrontal cortex in the brain, thus activating the brain into a happy, positive state.

Muster Up the Courage

Have you heard the phrase, "Feel the fear and do it anyway?" When we find the bravery and courage to just go for it, we often realize it wasn't as bad as we thought it would be. Visualize a positive outcome and to see the positive effects on your life.

Growth Mindset

Having a growth mindset means embracing challenges to improve one's life; it is a mindset wherein one always sees opportunity for growth.

This is the area to focus on. Expand the mind, welcome challenges, and embrace them as lessons to expand possibilities.

Be accepting of feedback that is constructive.

Be inspired by others who are leading the way. Embrace that as inspiration for yourself.

Understand that a setback is a moment to reflect and make changes. Know that there is no cap on what is possible. Always be open to learning and growing. It's an ever-evolving journey within.

Change Your Belief Systems

Belief systems are stories we tell ourselves to define our personal sense of reality. We all have belief systems that come from patterns in our past.

The good news is, we can alter them. We can reprogram our mindset to embrace new beliefs that are more positive. Without getting too scientific, understand that we have inner powers to make alterations, always. The true power is the willingness for change. Decide to define your beliefs according to your true core values.

Live a Life by Design

I have set out to live a life on purpose. Every day we have choices to live by design. Make life your own. Stop and smell the basil in your garden. Embark on a new adventure that fuels you. Find a hobby you want to explore. Embrace the value and beauty that surrounds you. Connect with nature. Always say "yes" to opportunities that speak to you. Walk the path that draws you toward connecting with your true desires and fulfilling them. Don't hold back. Life is so precious, start living your best life *now*.

Chapter 14
Untethered from the 'Should'

Nicole Woodcox Bolden

"Every day, our minds are collecting evidence for the case of self. The case that will push us to finally trust ourselves. Trust-in-self allows us to fly beyond our boldest dreams, and break free from the shoulds that keep us tethered to the ground. Let's fly!"

Hailing from the Windy City, Chicago-native Nicole Woodcox Bolden is an author and licensed clinical social worker with a mission to support parents in living more conscious lives so that they can not only raise healthy children, but also inspire their children to thrive. Nicole has authored a four-week workbook for mothers, created online courses, and has spoken on various platforms across the US, including NPR, Chicago Reader, Big City Moms conferences, and a multitude of social media outlets on the topic of maternal mental health.

When she's not holding safe and compassionate spaces for clients, you can find Nicole exploring in an RV with her two creative daughters and husband. Nicole and her family love a good adventure, laughing, eating popcorn, and having family game nights.

Nicole has a big mission of touching at least 10,000 families a year. To learn more about how you take part in this mission, connect with Nicole on her social media platforms and her website.

www.ThrivingwithBaby.com

ig: Thrivingwithbabychicago ~ fb: ThrivingwithBaby

li: thriving-with-baby

E very day we have to wake up and decide to live life, otherwise, we passively fall into catering to all the "shoulds" of our family, past circumstances, friends, bosses, bank accounts, and society. Falling into the world of the "shoulds" can be very deceptive because, most of the time, they pose as motivation, even while they're coiling around you like a boa constrictor. They squeeze you until, one day, when you are driving down a dark snow-covered road, you catch yourself thinking that it wouldn't be too bad if you slid into a ditch. Or your alarm goes off and you'd rather somehow disappear than get out of bed to start the workday. We know those thoughts are scary, but we shake them off because we don't have any active plans to end our lives. So we keep going, allowing the "shoulds" to continue to squeeze the joy out of our lives. Now, I know some of you may say that you are living your best life right now. I celebrate you and invite you to join me on my journey of discovery, just in case you have a friend who is hanging on by a thread. One of my internet mentors, Lisa Nichols, shares that every day we wake up possessing all that we need to make a daily extraordinary decision. "Should" thinking and extraordinary decision-making rarely reside in the same space. Therefore, I had to release some beliefs that were no longer serving me to get closer to realizing that idea. Let's take a short journey through understanding the basics of the "shoulds," some of my stories of how the "shoulds" show up in my life, and discuss some tools I have used to befriend my thoughts in a way that gives me the power to release the strings that tie me to the "shoulds."

Words are a powerful weapon that can encourage or discourage. Many of us try to be intentional with the words that we say to other people, but are flippant with the words that we say to ourselves. When we tell someone they "should" do a thing, we are typically trying to discourage a certain behavior, thus implying that there is a right and wrong way to behave in a situation. Whenever right and wrong are introduced to the thought cycle, shame has an easy path of entry to the party. Shame makes the "shoulds" heavy. The average person has good intentions when they share a "should," which makes the shame connected to the "shoulds" a particularly quiet and deadly mental weapon. "I should have known better" is a common foundational thought when trauma work happens in therapy. The distrust of self that is stirred up with this notion can keep us very close to a survival state of mind, because distrust of self does not feel safe. Can you see the vicious cycle that is kick-started with one seemingly simple word? Words are powerful. Word choices make a difference when the mind is craving permission to feel or heal. The ability to own your desires starts with the words you allow to influence you. Therefore, intentionality with our word choices is key when aiming to make extraordinary decisions that will lead to an untethered life of possibilities.

All day, every day, we are creating stories. Our brain does not like loose ends. Therefore, every day we are in a giant mad libs book. Mad Libs is that childhood game that some teachers use to teach kids how to use various parts of speech, where you have a template of a mostly completed story and you are tasked to fill in the blank spaces with words of your choice. Like Mad Libs, we are filling in gaps in our mental stories all day based on our current perspectives. This allows our minds to have a complete story in order to guide us in how to proceed, for the moment. When someone forgets to text us back, your partner added a little salt to the meal you just cooked, or your child is being extra sassy, our mind puts its own words into the story to try to make sense of the nonverbal interaction. So even though your partner told you they liked your meal after they ate it, it was too late for your brain to believe them. Your mind is already in defense mode due to the gap you filled in. Now all you can think is, "He hates my cooking. Why did I even try?" Then, your mind goes back to that one time your dad told you not to worry about cooking because you are smart and can hire a chef. Now, you aren't even mad about the salt your partner added, but you are upset that you don't have the money to hire a personal chef, and you feel like a failure. Yes, yes, that leap really happened to me. Don't judge!—you probably do it too. I just said it out loud. If only I had taken a quick pause to ask the question, "What am I telling myself about this situation right now?" and then actually waited to hear the answer. I may have been able to pump the brakes on that fast train to thoughts of failure. That train was sponsored by the "shoulds" of being a good wife that is great at all things around the house and that I "should" be in a certain financial place because I was a smart kid who received good grades in school. The way my mind made the leap about not being a good chef is one of the smaller representations of how being tied to "shoulds" can quickly make you question yourself. The shame that my version of being a wife didn't resemble what I had seen in my mother or on television, and the shame of not meeting society's standards for success were also present on that train. Being tethered to the "shoulds" at that time in my life made it hard for me to own my journey to building a family, which only shook up my mental health in ways that I could not have imagined.

There was a time in my life when I truly believed that I could change the world. The belief still lingers in my mind but it typically shows up in a smaller version, like, "I can inform my family and community." Other people's stories infiltrated some of my thought cycles, fueling the concept of imposter syndrome in all areas of my life. When I would look in the mirror, the image on the other side had literally changed. This shift was so dramatic that I went from a person who also saw a powerful, solid, and beautiful woman to seeing a morbidly obese slob. After having my kids, the stories and the "shoulds" started to squeeze me hard, spinning my mind out of control. I am a social worker by trade and have worked with young people for most of my career. So parenting should have come easy to me, right? I was involved and led multiple organizations while in school, so juggling work, family life, and all the other things in life should have been a breeze for me, right? Well, while dealing with postpartum depression and anxiety, those things felt like Herculean tasks. Passive suicidal ideation became a regular and scary thing for me during that time. These types of thoughts can take the form of intrusive images of you dying by some sort of accident (not necessarily by car, but not a natural death). But outside of the thoughts, you don't have any real plans to kill yourself. Please reach out for support if you are experiencing this. You are not alone. These thoughts are your mind trying to get your attention that something is not in alignment with your well-being. The time that was the scariest, and that kicked me out of the dangerous spiral enough to get some help, was when I was driving home one night with my babies in the back seat. It was a dark winter night and the snow was coming down hard. Out of nowhere, the idea of getting hit and spinning into the nearby ditch came into my mind. The image went all the way to me dying but my kids living without me. At that point, I realized I needed help.

When I reached out for help, I was reminded that our ruminations are not facts, that mental wellness is not about waging war on yourself. It's about learning how to befriend your thoughts in order to understand their communication style. Our mind is always trying to communicate a need to protect us. Therefore, it is vital to give ourselves some mental space by welcoming our feelings in as signals. I was reminded that I was in survival mode. My people-pleasing was a toxic trauma response because it was coming from a place of fear instead of kindness. Our childhood brings about many memories and expectations of life. Sometimes, these memories are positive and they give us a solid foundation for creating our own family. Other times, these memories are not so good, maybe even traumatic. If these memories are traumatic, it can mess with the confidence that we are trying to build in adulthood. This lack of confidence can get us tethered to all the arbitrary "shoulds" that society has in store because we are searching for permission or validation outside of ourselves.

Now that we have journeyed through what the "shoulds" are and seen some examples of how they play out in real life, let's talk tools. Although "should" can quickly spiral us into survival mode, we do not need to fear it. Reframing our relationship with our mind will give us more room in between our thoughts, emotions, and actions. Our thinking process has a few stages that can feel like one big stage if we aren't mindful. The first tool I will share with you is the thought, emotion, action cycle from cognitive behavioral therapy. This tool reminds us that awareness is one of the most important steps when it comes to living a life that is in alignment with our most authentic self. This cycle makes us aware that our thoughts, emotions, and actions are all separate entities, even though they highly influence each other. Which means we have more power than we give ourselves credit for in most situations. Having concerns about disappointing a parent does not have to automatically equal having the emotions of disappointment, embarrassment, or sadness. Just like having the idea of quitting your job doesn't automatically equal the action of walking out of your place of employment. Since we are now aware that our thoughts and actions are separate, the concern of disappointing a parent can actually spark the emotion of curiosity, encouraging our mind to find more evidence to remind us that our parents' love is not tied to our achievements.

Here are some tools to help you befriend your thoughts.

Create power pauses with the You Are ENOUGH checklist:

- Energy—Where are your energy levels? Have you eaten? How did you sleep?

- No—What do you need to say *no* to today?

- Outside—How can you get outside, or talk to someone positive outside of your immediate family?

- Understanding—How can you give yourself a little bit of grace today?

- Grateful—What went right today? What are you grateful for today?

- Happy—What is one thing you can do today to make yourself smile?

Create your mental safe space:

1. Do some quick physical movement (e.g., jumping jacks, running in place, shaking your body one limb at a time, like the hokey pokey dance). This movement is a quick way to try to complete the stress response cycle and help your mind/body get out of survival mode. It is important to try to complete the stress response cycle as much as possible before creating your mental or even physical

safe space, so that you can have a little more clarity to truly honor your needs at the moment. To dive deeper into stress response cycles, read the book, *Burnout: The Secret to Unlocking the Stress Cycle,* by Amelia and Emily Nagoski.

2. Think about what things, situations, or people bring joy.

3. Think about what things, situations, or people you feel the most authentic around.

4. Write the names of any things, situations, or people that overlap from questions 2 and 3.

5. Now, create one place, mentally, where you can be fully present with the things or people from question 4. In order for this mental safe space to stick, it is helpful to describe this place fully out loud, like via voice memo, or even sign language.

6. Try utilizing this mental safe space a few times while actively relaxing your body. This will help create a positive association with the mental safe space. Please note that it is okay if you have to create multiple safe spaces.

The main reasons I encourage people to create mental safe spaces are to assist the mind and body to come out of survival mode, and to use the space as a grounding point to examine if you are honoring yourself in a certain moment. It can also serve as a reference point for how you need to be nurtured in this current season of life. The mental safe space reminds us that it is okay for you to take up space in your mind and life. All of these things guide you towards more authentic living, thus leaving behind the chains of the "shoulds." The "shoulds" will still show up from time to time, but they will be fleeting thoughts instead of ones that feel like boulders on your chest.

Embrace the silent pauses that these exercises bring. There are many answers that can be heard when you finally slow down to listen to your authentic self and not the self that has been "should" on by family and society. These silent pauses helped me to realize that I had started to take a back seat in my own life. That I was holding on to a belief that being a good mother and wife meant self-sacrificing. My mind didn't truly believe this idea and was literally trying to escape them with the thoughts of me dying. The next time you feel a case of the "shoulds" coming on, remind yourself that this is a signal to check in with yourself. You can check in to see why this survival state of mind is showing up at this moment. Go to your safe space and breathe your way to the response that will serve you the most in that situation. Saying "no," asking for help, or taking breaks do not make you weak. They are signs of self-love. Once you start to truly love yourself, playing small stops being an option.

Chapter 15

Everyone Has a Story

Christa Greenland

"Life is a series of small moments strung together to create something bigger."

Christa Greenland is a wife, mother of two children, an entrepreneur, and a coffee addict. She grew up in a small town north of Toronto, Ontario with her parents and two older brothers. In high school, she always had the desire to create her own life and be her own boss. It took her many years to make this desire a reality. She became an entrepreneur in 2015 when she joined the network marketing company Epicure, where she helped others put good food on the table while reducing stress and saving time. Through this journey, she learned the importance of self-discovery, which unlocked her passions and her calling in life. This led her to launch The Minted Green Company in 2019, a space where she is passionate about helping others find their authentic voice so that they can create an impact in the online world. She believes everyone has a story to tell and that someone out there is waiting to hear it!

www.themintedgreencompany.com ~ www.christagreenland.com

ig: themintedgreencompany, christagreenland

li: linkedin.com/in/themintedgreencompany

Hope. A four-letter word that can make all the difference in how you see the world around you. Is it full of life and potential, or confusion and heartache? When you think of your life and where you are in this moment, what do you see?

I know what it is like to have no hope. To feel lost and unsure of which way to turn. Do you go left or do you go right? The options feel so empty that you just stay in place because it is easier than making a decision.

Life has a way of moving us through the seasons, and when we don't pay attention, we may not even realize that time has passed.

My story didn't start off as a hopeless one. It was filled with hope, love, joy, and life. I come from a loving home with parents who love me, but it was not without its challenges. There was one specific moment that impacted and changed my life forever. When I think about that day, I can remember it so clearly. I can still see all the details of our kitchen, like the white cupboards and blue countertops, while all five of us (my parents, my two older brothers, and myself) gathered to hear what my parents wanted to share. Having open communication in our family was very important to them. Now, you're probably wondering, "What did they tell you?" and I wish I could share those details, but that isn't my story to tell.

My parents had no idea that what they shared impacted each of us differently. Even if they had decided not to share it with us, the atmosphere in our home had changed while they worked through all the pain, frustration, and stress to receive the healing that they needed. This, however, was the beginning of my journey, and it would be years—almost twenty-five years—before I received true healing from that moment.

At twelve years old, there wasn't much that I was able to do. I didn't understand the stress, so I did the only thing that I could do: I subconsciously began to control my food. This was the beginning of my struggle with food, my struggle with an eating disorder. This was when I stopped eating every time things got difficult. When I did eat, I gravitated towards foods that were high in sugar, anything deep fried, and nothing good for me.

As a teenager struggling with an eating disorder, I also struggled with depression, anxiety, and suicidal thoughts. I was lost. I was numb. I had no idea who I was or who I was called to be. I wanted to be invisible; I truly tried to be invisible. I would sit in the back of the classroom, never raising my hand, never participating. I would never eat lunch in the lunchroom.

I continued to spiral through the pain and I was out of control. I had started smoking cigarettes when I was fourteen years old and I completely defied my parents' rules. Many people assumed I was being rebellious. What they didn't realize was that I was hurting and I truly wanted to be seen. It was a cry for help.

These unhealthy patterns continued for ten years. It wasn't until my early twenties that things began to change.

I had given up. I was at the end of the line. I had no interest in life. I turned to alcohol, my drinking had become excessive but still controlled. I was balancing myself on a fine line that could tip at any moment and I didn't care. There was nothing left in this life that gave me hope. I was doing the same thing, day in and day out. I tried constantly to bury the pain, to control it, but I never succeeded. It was always there.

Around that same time, my parents invited me to a church service that was different from anything I'd experienced as a child. During that service, I saw hope. I had been searching for hope for years and now it was there, waiting for me. The following week, I received an invitation to build a relationship with Jesus, something that was completely foreign to me. I grew up in the church and learned nothing about having a relationship with Him. But the thoughts that went through my head were, "Let's give this a try. It can't hurt anymore than I already do." The moment that I said "yes," I could feel the weight being lifted from my shoulders, the burden of all those years being taken away. It was so freeing.

I want to tell you that my challenges and struggles didn't go away at that moment. They were still there, but it was different.

Instead of despair, I had hope. Instead of depression, I had joy. Instead of fear, I had life. My path in life had changed. I was on the road of recovery. I am still walking on that path, even to this day.

If I hadn't said "yes" to Jesus that day, I would probably be dead right now. Those ten years of darkness have given me so much understanding and gratitude for the light. And when I reflect on them, I wouldn't change a thing. Those challenges and struggles that I experienced have shaped me into the woman that I am today. However, my journey didn't end here. It was just the beginning of healing, learning, understanding, and discovering who I am.

Do you believe that the small moments in our lives impact us? We know that the big ones do, but what about the little ones? Those things that happened all the way back in our early childhood. Decisions that we made, words that were spoken to us, self-judgment. It wasn't until 2018, when I truly jumped into the journey toward finding out who I am, that I realized how much those small moments had impacted me. Like I tell my kids, every decision we make has a consequence. It can be good or bad. Some of those decisions may have been out of our control. However, what we do decide is how we react in those kinds of situations. This is what impacts us. This is what can change the path that we are on.

I ended up on a path of self-discovery and it showed me so much. I discovered that I used food as a source of control, to control how I looked at myself, how I felt, my emotions, my outlook in life, and so many other things. I didn't think that I was fat and needed to lose weight. I was just not confident in who I was and what I had to offer. It was visible in how I carried myself. I did not stand up tall. I stood with my shoulders slouched, trying to hide from the world.

I wasn't able to understand how I'd seen myself then, until I had truly moved out of the darkness and into the light. Being aware of how much we allow external things to dictate who we are and what we do is so important. When I think back to who I was before my journey of self-discovery began, I know that I wouldn't recognize that person today. Timid, meek, quiet, shy, all the things that I am not. My inner strength was hidden so well that I didn't even know that it existed. Those ten dark years tried to destroy the person that I am called to be. They tried to rob me of my value and worth, to silence my voice. And they may have been successful for a short period of time, but they didn't keep me down. They made me stronger, bolder, and even more confident.

What I find amusing is that in 2015, I joined Epicure, a network marketing company that sells food products. I don't love food, yet I earn an income cooking dinner. However, I am super grateful for Epicure. Shortly after I attended my first Epicure conference in August 2016, I was having coffee with a new friend and fellow consultant. We were chatting about why we joined Epicure. As I shared with her my story, or what I believed to be my story, she pushed me for more, as if she could tell that there was a missing part. It was then that I shared the details of my eating disorder out loud for the first time. In that moment, my voice became free, as if it had been chained shut prior to that moment. I decided that I was going to start talking about my journey and my relationship with food. Eating disorders, for many people, often hide struggles, ones that we try to bury and not talk about. They keep us in the dark, handcuffed to our pain. They keep us lonely and numb. Only when we speak out do we break free from those chains. That is what happened to me.

Even as I write this, I still can't believe where my journey has taken me. I never imagined being able to build a healthy relationship with food while sharing my struggles with others. Slowly, I talked about my eating disorder in cooking classes and in front of groups of people. It was both scary and empowering. Each time, at least one person came up to me afterward to share the story of their experience with an eating disorder. It made me realize this problem is much more common than we think.

Being honest about my journey has opened up doors that I would have never expected. Through telling my story publicly at events, I met Linda Brown, who shared with me that she too has struggled with eating properly and would often skip breakfast. This started our relationship of swapping breakfast food photos. Those morning check-ins are precious to me. They help me stay on track. Having people become part of your journey is so important to being able to move forward. I know she is always there for me and that I can connect with her when times are difficult. Surrounding yourself with people who've got your back will make all the difference in achieving what you are working towards.

As I navigated through my self-discovery journey, I realized that something was missing. It was a key part of who I was called to be. It was my voice, my story, and the realization that there were people in the world who had similar challenges to what I went through. They needed validation and to know that they were not alone.

Do you believe your experiences are important and that there is someone out there waiting to hear what you have to say? We have the ability to change people's lives, and it is much simpler than you might expect. It is your story. There is power behind your story. Others want to know that they are not alone in their challenges. They want to know that someone else has walked this path and made it through. This is the reason I jumped at the opportunity to share my story here. I know that someone needs to hear it, and that person might be you.

When I look at the world today, I realize that there are so many different ways to share our stories. Social media is an important one that gives us the opportunity to connect with people around the world. It was the reason that The Minted Green Company was born. I wanted to help people find their authentic voice in the online world so that they can create an impact. I have the privilege of helping many people to rediscover themselves, their voice, and their message. When was the last time you shared your story? What is the message that is in your heart that you want to share? Life is a series of small moments strung together to create something bigger. Those small moments, the snippets of your life, have a greater impact that you can ever imagine. Break free from the bondage that is holding you back and share your journey!

It is amazing how much I allowed moments that are out of my control to impact who I was meant to be. But do you want to know something crazy? I wouldn't change any of it. That moment, in my family's kitchen, when I was twelve years old, has shaped me into the person who I am today. It is so important to embrace who you are and all the things that you have been through because they helped mold you into who you are today. When we embrace those moments, we open up and allow healing to happen. This is when we can shine our light for others.

Do you believe that everything you have gone through has shaped who you are today? Think about all those moments in time that have impacted your journey. Many times, we don't realize that the things we experienced as children have shaped the person who we are in this moment. I challenge you to spend some time reflecting on your life. Yes, this can be difficult but I promise you it is worth it. Are you ready for change? Do you want hope in your life? Do you want to be a voice for those who can't speak? If you said "yes" to any of those questions, you need to spend some time thinking about where you have been. Not just the big moments that impacted your life, but also the little ones. There are people who want to know that they are not alone in their journey and you have an authentic voice and story that can impact their lives. They need to hear your story. Be an agent of change!

Chapter 16
The Lifeline I Didn't Know I Needed

Julie Clark Wobbe

"When we come from a place of having worked through our dark, we
create space to love ourselves, our people, and our homes,
in the light."

Julie is a magical unicorn, passionate about helping women to believe in themselves, find their light, and lead with love and grace. She believes kindness will change the world, and it starts with each of us. When we pour into ourselves, we naturally pour into others.

Julie is humbled to be one of the coauthors of *Uncover Your Light*. Through life's lessons, she has experienced many revelations, one among them is that many of the stories we have been told—or even tell ourselves—are not true.

Julie is a Decluttering Mindset Coach, assisting families in releasing their attachment to their stuff and finding joy, creating space in their hearts, their homes and their lives. Julie lives in Ontario with her two children affectionately referred to as the beans. They also share their home with a bearded dragon, two kittens, and a litter of bunnies. She loves to spend time outdoors in nature collecting rocks. When she's inside, you'll often find her in the kitchen baking for her friends and family.

www.creatingspacewithjulie.com

ig: _creatingspacewithjulie ~ fb: creatingspacewithjulie

li: Julie Clark Wobbe

Hello, friend. Yes, you, beautiful reader. I encourage you, at this moment, to pause, to look around. How do you feel? What can you smell? What do you hear? Now look at your beautiful surroundings, find gratitude, notice the things that make you smile, and recall the memories that bring you joy, hope, comfort, love . . . just for a moment, be with only yourself and your life.

How Do You Feel?

A huge part of uncovering my light has been the realization that I am enough, and that the stories I used to tell myself are not true. I have learned that when I pause, allowing myself the time and space to feel, my heart opens, I see life through gratitude, love, and abundance. I hope that by sharing part of my journey, it will inspire you and help you uncover your light.

"The wound is the place where the light enters you." -Rumi

A year after my marriage ended, I walked into the kitchen and saw that my dishwasher was leaking. I then started crying, over my sink. I did not think I had any tears left, but I did. At that moment, I felt scared and like I couldn't keep doing this. This was hard, I didn't know where to start, I hadn't asked to do this alone, and I wanted someone to come in and save me.

My children found me and they froze; I knew they felt scared and worried about me. I was the only adult they had and I felt broken. Seeing them, I knew I had to get through this. I was the one who could save me. I wanted to show them that we could do this together. They helped me realize that we could break the generational cycle of always feeling "not good enough."

Soon after this moment at the kitchen sink, a friend made an observation that has stuck with me ever since. Sitting in our dining room, she said, "Jules, your home looks the same as it did when your husband lived here. You haven't changed anything and it feels like he still lives here." Looking around, she then asked, "Do you even like the color brown? There is a lot of brown. Maybe it's time to paint it a color that you like?"

She was right. Aside from moving the television up from the basement, I had not changed anything else in the entire house.

When I thought about making changes, I felt guilty, and I was afraid of what the changes would stir up. Would my children think I was erasing our past memories? Would it hurt their dad's feelings? Would friends help? Did I have time? Was I even capable of doing this on my own? This was the first time I had lived on my own, and I wanted to make the home *feel* like my own, but fear was stopping me. Up until then, I had never worked on home improvements. I'd felt judged and was told "no" for so long that my confidence was very low and, at times, I felt paralyzed by the fear of making changes and the worry that I might make a mess of it.

To help remedy this fear, I connected to my heart and asked for a sign, and then this incredible feeling of light came over me.

Why are you holding onto this story that you are not enough? Why are you focusing on the dark, on all the things that could go wrong? What about all the shifts you have made, the love you have? What about the people who are here and want to help? What if you believed in yourself?

I was inspired to start, and my children were on board. We talked about how we wanted to feel in our home and what we wanted to work on. Our wish list included a bubble spa, painting the bedrooms, and rethinking the main floor, which was the first space we wanted to tackle since we spent most of our time there. One of my friends had installed a gorgeous silver and crystal light fixture in her dining room. We found something similar for our space. That was the first change we made, and it brought joy to our hearts and home. It was new and bright, sparkling with crystals, and it felt like magic.

We started to make a list of the things we could change that wouldn't cost a lot of money and that were important to us. My children wanted to work on their bedrooms and I wanted to continue with our living room. I focused on the fireplace, I had dreams of painting it white.

A few days later, I walked into a paint store and asked if they could suggest a paint for a brick fireplace. I showed them photos and explained my vision. Armed with suggestions and lots of encouragement, I brought the paint home and I started. It took three days and was worth every moment. Even the people who doubted me had to admit—it looked good.

Another friend helped us create an inspirational accent wall. With each new project, we continued to ask ourselves how we wanted to feel and almost always our answer was "joyful," so that became our theme.

Our next project was painting the walls. Most of them were beige, and we all agreed that we wanted to change them. I let my children choose the paint for their bedrooms. My youngest chose pink and my oldest chose gray. I loved pink and knew I wanted a pink and white bathroom. When we were in the paint store, the consultant asked if I was sure about the paint color for the bathroom, and did I realize it was pink. At that moment, I started to second guess myself, until I remembered that I got to choose. I said, "Yes, we are painting the bathroom pink."

After we painted, we re-arranged the furniture and bought new duvets and pillows. Our bedrooms became places where each of us could see our personalities reflected.

One of my favorite projects was our photo wall, where we hung photos of friends and family and moments that brought us joy. It's a daily reminder that our home is filled with love and that we are supported.

In the midst of making changes, the energy inside of me changed, too. I felt lighter and more confident. I was filled with gratitude and leaned towards the light. It felt like a cloud had been lifted from my life, and friends and family noticed. They often shared with us how proud they were and how they felt joy in our space too.

This was great, except I had a secret. I loved clearing and creating space. I worked on spaces easily but I wasn't dealing with the emotions attached to our space. I moved stuff to the basement to create the upstairs I wanted and the basement was piling up. I tried to forget about it, pretend it wasn't there. I spent all of my time upstairs or in the backyard. This worked until I had to call in a repair person. As he walked downstairs I joked that I would come looking if he didnt come back. He smiled, but I was embarrassed. All the shame I had been hiding filled my head. Unresolved feelings around my marriage, the resentment I felt about being left with all the stuff, not to mention all of the shopping I had done for years as a way to soothe my unhappiness, it started to feel overwhelming. I was living a double life, upstairs was a bright and happy space filled with joy, and the basement made me feel like I was drowning in physical and emotional clutter.

Around that time, a friend sent me a text inviting me to join a five-day decluttering challenge with her. We had never talked about our clutter before, so how did she know that I needed help? Was my secret out? It turns out, she didn't know, but she was getting value out of the challenge and thought I would too.

I loved the challenge. The women who participated were just like me, wanting to be free of the shame attached to clutter. One of the principles that struck me was the idea that we are not our stuff. Stuff is just stuff; it doesn't define us as a person.

No one had described clutter in this way to me before. I decided to test this idea while going through our stuff. When I looked through a box, or a shelf, or even a complete room, I no longer saw a mess. Now, for the first time, instead of seeing all of those things and feeling the darkness come over me, I saw an opportunity to create space for more lightness in my life. In those five days, I worked through more clutter than I had in my entire life. I loved the community and I was learning so much. The more I decluttered, the less I wanted to buy, and this started a ripple effect. I felt more confident, and this sparked the idea of feeling like I was enough, right now, in the moment, not when my home looked like a magazine, or when I found love, or when someone told me I was enough. Right then I started to believe in myself. Decluttering was the lifeline I didn't know that I needed.

Open Your Heart to Receiving

One of the ideas I was still struggling with was love: self-love and being loved. When my marriage ended, I internalized the breakup as a sign that I wasn't enough. I was able to love others, but I felt that my heart was closed to receiving love, from myself and others. There were moments in my life when receiving love seemed possible, but then, I would get stuck on all the reasons I felt I was unworthy. As I focused more on decluttering, the energy around me changed. I did more of the things that brought me joy, and my heart started to open to the possibilities of love.

I continued decluttering, adding in meditation and journal practice. I wrote letters of forgiveness, I read them out loud and then I burned them. I embraced my authentic self, all of me, even the parts I had wanted to hide. In the process of decluttering our stuff, I changed my mindset, my heart was opened, my relationships deepened, and love found me.

I learned that love comes in many forms: The love and grace I have for myself, the love I have for my children, my friends, and our family, the communities I belong to, and romantic love. Not the Cinderella story I grew up with, but the kind of love where both of you are whole, and when together, you feel like you are home. This happened unexpectedly and also at the moment it was supposed to, at a time when I believed I was worthy the way I was and that I was always enough.

Creating Space

A few months later, I was presented with an opportunity to train to become a decluttering coach. While I didn't know how, I knew why. I was being called to invest in myself so I could hold space for others, a safe space to help them see their worth, their gifts, and release the shame they have been holding onto.

The idea that there could be another way to look at our homes, removing the shame, finding the joy, had become a part of me. I needed to share this. I wanted to create a safe place that allowed others to work on their beliefs around clutter, feeling supported, and applying skills to their space, on their timeline. I wanted them to know that they could choose how they felt in their homes, and that I could help them uncover their light. I felt all of this, and one thing was still holding me back. My children. I feared that I was already busy and that this extra commitment would take even more time away from them, so I asked the universe for a sign.

"Mom, you should do this," my twelve-year-old, who I call Bean, told me. "What I have felt is that when you do things that make you happy, fill your cup, things that bring you joy, our family works better, and we are all happier." This was my sign. My Bean saw what I couldn't see myself. Taking time for me and doing the things that brought me joy wasn't taking time away from them, it was adding to it! They were showing me that when I filled my cup, I naturally poured it into others. This was a beautiful full circle moment for me.

When we declare what we want, when we take action, the universe matches our energy. I believe I manifested that for us.

Four months later, I was a professional decluttering mindset coach.

I am so grateful for all of the beautiful souls I have had the absolute pleasure of working with. Their vulnerability and willingness to allow me into their lives, hold space, and encourage them, is such a blessing. In the process of decluttering our home, I had opened my heart to service and abundance.

I became a decluttering coach because I knew in my heart and in my soul that my purpose was to hold space for others and help them open their hearts to the possibility of light. By providing a safe space to help them see their worth and their gifts, they are able to release the shame they have been holding onto.

We Need the Light and the Dark

When I am triggered, I lean towards the dark. In those moments, I remind myself that I am okay, we are okay, we have been here before, and we know what to do. We are kinder to ourselves, we love more, and we can pause and find something to be grateful for. I learned to give myself permission to feel all the feelings, the light and the dark, without judgment.

I believe that while I would never wish any of my pain on another, I understand it better now. Those chapters of my life needed to be opened, read, healed, loved, and released. I have accepted all of me and embraced it because it made me the person I am today.

There came a time when I needed to figure out what to release to step into my light.

What if I believed that I was enough, in this moment, that no matter what happened or will happen, I am truly enough? That life happens for me, not to me.

Friends, I encourage you, every single day, to find a moment, to practice the pause, with gratitude. Believe in and love yourself by giving yourself time to forgive, heal, be open, and remember to take time for you to uncover your light.

Chapter 17
Listening to Your Inner Voice

Carol Ward

"I believe we are the creators of our own journey. We may get distracted along the way, and by listening to our inner voice, we are led home."

Carol is a Money Mindset Mentor with a passion for helping women peel away their limiting beliefs and experience an abundant life.

As she journeys through this ever-changing life, she is blessed to have by her side her soulmate of over twenty years, and their two lovely teenagers. She enjoys walking along the beautiful trails in Markham, Ontario, meditating in the morning, writing in her journal, expressing her gratitude at night, and reading on her Kindle. Continuous self-growth is important to Carol, and she is always looking for ways to expand her knowledge.

Carol is currently leading a women's group, FemCity Richmond Hill Collective, and is grateful to connect and engage with like-minded women who support each other with positivity, trust, and gratitude.

While Carol enjoyed many years working as an accountant, she felt a calling to work on her inner beliefs. She is now certified as a master NLP (Neuro Linguistic Practitioner) practitioner and uses her knowledge and experience to empower women to look at their finances with confidence and clarity.

She was guided out of the darkness of her own self-limiting beliefs that were holding her back, and is now living an amazing life of endless possibilities!

www.mindsenze.com

ig: carolwardcpa ~ fb: carol.ward.555

li: coach-carol-ward-cpa

There is one thing I am sure of: everything that happens in this life has a purpose. Through every experience, there is always an opportunity to learn, grow, and evolve. No matter which stage of life you are in, challenges allow for lessons to be learned.

As I look back at my life, one thing that stands out is my unwavering faith. My belief in God has provided me joy in the good times, and also comfort in situations where I encountered adversity. It has provided me with a sort of "knowing" that can ease my soul and lead me through turbulent times. I like to call this "knowing" my inner voice. No matter what your belief system is, your inner voice is there, and it is one of the most powerful tools you have been gifted with.

Through the years of learning about my inner voice, I recognized that it is often difficult to know where to start. Sometimes, I found myself pushing back, not ready for what my inner voice was telling me. Maybe I wasn't ready for the impending change, or in some cases, maybe I didn't *want* it. Through my experiences, I came to understand that my inner voice was simply me, the me that was in tune with my soul. It was only when I accepted my intuition that it could flourish, and in turn, so could I.

I am so grateful to have the opportunity to share my story and reflect on the times I learned to communicate with my inner voice. It has guided me out of the darkness and into the light. Along the way, I learned to recognize when my inner voice was trying to get my attention, the best ways to receive those messages, and how to express my gratitude for this amazing power.

It started off as any normal day in October 2010. It was a Sunday morning. I woke up and began to get myself ready. It was then that I noticed that the small lump I had on my breast had started to hurt. Feeling a little concerned, I visited the emergency room.

They're just going to tell me everything is fine, I thought. *Carol, you're just making a big deal over nothing.*

After countless tests, needles, biopsies, and surgeries, it was confirmed: That unassuming lump was DCIS: stage 0 cancer. All I could think was: "How did I get here?" I had a cancer diagnosis.

I remember feeling helpless, anxious, and scared at first. I was in a dazed state of disbelief for two days. I prayed, I asked for help, and pleaded for the opportunity to watch my children grow up. I prayed for clarity, and for a chance to remain on this earth. On the third day, I felt better and more positive. Although I was scared, I somehow knew everything was going to be okay. This was my intuition communicating with me. I had a deep sense of knowing, a certainty I felt in my soul, that I was on the path of recovery. Feeling calm and peaceful, my body started the healing process. I was grateful for my friends and family who showed up with delicious home-cooked meals, words of comfort, and laughter. Spending this time with my family and friends helped to take my mind off my worries, and instead, allowed me to be in the present moment and enjoy their stories.

For me, thinking positively was essential. My prognosis was good; the cancer had not progressed, and it was still in the DCIS stage, which is the earliest form of breast cancer, and is non-invasive. I could not succumb to the hopeless feelings. Maintaining a positive mindset, however, was tricky at times. Sometimes, mostly at night, my mind was all over the place and I couldn't properly tune into my inner voice. I continued to pray and asked for guidance.

At nighttime, when the world was asleep, I was awake. Even at two in the morning, my mind would race to the point that I couldn't sleep. I remember listening to CDs of running water every night to quiet my anxious thoughts. This type of meditation, while simple, was extremely soothing, and I was able to peacefully go back to sleep. Night after night, I would listen and meditate on the running water, and sleeping became easier and easier. I was calm, I could concentrate once again, and my inner voice was becoming clearer. During the day, I could employ the technique of visualization to help heal my mind. I would visualize my doctor telling me that I had been healed, and I would focus on how this news made me feel.

Looking back, I recognize the lesson in letting go of the ego, asking for help, and surrendering to the answers. My inner voice was there, leaping off the sidelines and right into the center of my mind. Using these tools allowed my mind to be calm and free from any worries, fear, or anxiety in the present moment. It is my belief that I had to let go and surrender in the current moment so that my body could recover. Now that I was able to hear and recognize my inner voice, the next step was to learn to implement these messages.

After becoming certified as a mindset coach, it was easier for me to be aware of my intuitive messages. One of the first things I noticed was that we live in a fear-based culture. We're terrified of uncertainty and are constantly anticipating the worst. We are so accustomed to living our lives based on our unconscious habits and beliefs, we rarely question whether they are serving us positively or negatively. I also notice that sometimes when there is a big question to ask or an important decision to make, we tend to look outside of ourselves for the answers. We may get advice from our friends and family, read books, or ask the experts. Yet, we often neglect to check with the most important thing, which is our own intuition. Whether we want to make better decisions or solve problems faster, tuning in to our intuition and listening to our inner wisdom will help us achieve these results.

I am grateful that once again, I listened to my inner voice and explored the possibility of changing my career. I had studied for many years and put my whole being into attaining my chartered professional accountant certification. I loved my work. Once my children were born, I placed my career on hold to be a stay-at-home mom, always with the intention of returning to my life as an accountant. Eventually, the kids grew up, and I found I was no longer passionate about what was once my dream career. There was something inside me, a whisper of sorts, that told me to explore the power of mindset. I wanted out of my career, but I didn't know how to take that leap until I studied and became certified as an NLP master practitioner. Learning about the power of the mind and the effective use of language when speaking to ourselves and others was a game-changer for me. I realized we can choose our thoughts and beliefs, which lead to our actions and result in something powerful and exciting. It inspired me to take the steps to become a Money Mindset and Business Mentor. I feel a sense of fulfillment when my clients have their "ah-ha!" moment, change their limiting beliefs, and confidently manage their finances. I am once again passionate about my career and my purpose.

Intuition shows up in different ways for different people. For example, you may receive visual messages, such as images that appear in quick flashes or visions. Alternatively, you might receive your guidance as a hunch, a thought, or in words. Your intuition may communicate in a physical form, such as goosebumps, or a gut feeling. Sometimes intuitive messages are simply a sense of knowing and certainty. If you've ever felt that you knew something to be true in your soul, most likely, it was a message from your wisdom.

For me, intuition shows up predominantly as a sense of knowing and a feeling of rightfulness. I had this feeling when the opportunity to lead a women's networking group showed up in 2018. Initially, I was nervous to lead this group, but after meeting the ladies of the FemCity Richmond Hill Collective, I shifted that energy to excitement. And what a journey it has been! Everyone is supportive of each other and open to learning and sharing their knowledge in an environment filled with positivity and gratitude. As a global member, I teach classes and I am also included in panel discussions based on my expertise. Taking on this leadership role has been a success story for me!

Here are some methods to increase the volume of your intuition so you can effectively listen and trust it:

1. Meditate: Spending time in silence will quiet your mind and help you hear and interpret your intuitive messages easier and more efficiently. I normally meditate every morning for about ten minutes. This helps calm my mind and body.

2. Creativity: Engaging in creative activities, such as vision boarding, writing, or journaling, quiets the cognitive mind and allows your intuition to be heard. I write in my journal daily, since for me, it is a highly effective way to

access my intuition. I normally journal for just five to ten minutes, and I am amazed by the clarity of what comes through.

3. Clarity in Calmness: Have you ever had those "ah-ha!" moments when you're in the shower or driving your car? I have them all the time, especially in the shower. For me, running water is soothing and calms my mind. When I allow my mind to rest, it opens and allows my thoughts and emotions to flow through. I am surprised at the information that I receive. You will find that your intuition speaks to you when you are less busy, when you are calm, and when you are asleep.

4. Release Bad Feelings: Negative emotions will cloud intuition, which is why it's easier to make poor decisions when you're angry or upset. When I am feeling low, I count to ten, sometimes even fifteen, before I speak or make a decision. Overall, people make better choices when they are in a positive mood compared to when they are in a negative state.

Learning about the power of the mind was a game-changer for me. I believe we are born knowing we are powerful, and through our thoughts, we are the creators of our experiences. Along the way, I may have put this realization aside as I adopted other, less empowering beliefs.

Like many of us, I've had to move my workshops over to Zoom this past year. Unbelievably, for most of them, my computer would act up *just* as I was getting ready to start. From freezing, to the volume not working, it was like I was experiencing every problem in the book. While the problems were not tough to fix, it did raise my anxiety level. To combat this, I created a routine: Show up ten minutes early, make sure everything works, and resolve any problems. For a while, my routine was helping, but nevertheless, more problems arose. I decided to consult a life coach. I realized that in this case, my routine was a temporary fix, like using a Band-Aid, and I needed to find the source of the problem. Lo-and-behold, it was me! Even though I had found a good solution, unconsciously, I still had the old belief that my computer malfunctions would continue. The universe heard what I was focusing on and delivered it to me. Subsequently, I changed my belief and now had the expectation that my computer would work. And it did! The following week, I had two presentations and my computer worked beautifully, just like I expected it to. Even though we may consciously plan for a particular outcome, ultimately the result is determined by our beliefs playing in the background.

Today I am grateful to be reunited with this powerful belief, as it has changed my life in so many positive ways. The first step was the awakening, remembering my personal power and my reason for being here, which allowed me to gain control of my own destiny. In every moment, I can choose to focus positively or negatively. By deliberately reframing my thoughts, I am creating my life and changing my story. I've noticed that, over time, as I focus on the desired goal with positivity, I've experienced a shift in the way I feel about the subject. It is important to note that if you speak about something you desire, but you are feeling doubt about your own words, then the words will not bring you what you want. This is because the way you feel is the true indication of the direction of your thoughts or vibration and will lead to your results. Focus your thoughts on what you want, and this repetition will attract opportunity into your life.

Currently, I am very excited to have done many successful IGTV interviews, and to lead an amazing course that helps my members overcome their limiting beliefs, manage their finances, and live a life filled with positive thoughts. I am continuously looking for reasons to feel good, as this will attract other good feelings and place me in alignment with my inner self. While this may seem counterintuitive, it is important to notice when you are feeling negative emotions. This acts like a signal to let you know where you are right now and that it is time to change to positive thoughts and emotions. Shifting your mindset and being present right here, right now, will put you back in alignment with your inner voice.

My purpose is to inspire us to think positively, listen to our intuition, and to deliberately choose our thoughts so we can become the creators of our own life. When faced with adversity, ask for help, surround yourself with positive friends and family, and focus on thinking uplifting, healing thoughts. Your intuitive side will naturally become stronger when you are open, positive, and grateful. Expressing gratitude and practicing affirmations while feeling the emotions will empower you on your journey. By listening to my inner voice, I made powerful choices to change my career, take on a leadership role, and live my life knowing my outcome is based on my choices. I hope that my stories have been helpful and inspired you to be the creator of your own life.

Chapter 18
The Gift of Giving

Marcia Agius

"The meaning of life is to find your gift. The purpose of life is to give it away."

Marcia Agius is happily married to her best friend and has three wonderful kids. She spent the last twenty-five years in three different countries, running a busy household. Raising kids and supporting a hardworking husband was not always easy, but she always felt it was worth it. She feels proud to play such an important role in her family's successes and the lives they've built.

Over the years, many amazing women have inspired her, which prompted her to start Inspire Always, a forum that highlights and features incredible women showing their strengths and struggles. It's a community of women who motivate each other and cheer others on. It is a place that spreads kindness and positivity, especially during these trying times in the middle of a pandemic.

Philanthropy has always been a huge part of her life, and by starting Inspire Always, she has kept giving back. Marcia was a part of a major fund-raising campaign for Sunnybrook's Odette Cancer Center. She has also been involved with 100 Women Who Care, an organization that supports local charities in her community. Annually, she works closely with Make A Wish Foundation, granting wishes for special children. Most recently, she has partnered with a local organization, Million Dollar Smiles, which also grants wishes for children. Marcia connected to this charity through her community of inspiring women and she helped raise proceeds through the sale of t-shirts that spread her message to "Spread Kindness."

www.inspirealways.ca

ig: _inspirealways

"For it is in giving that we receive."
-St. Francis of Assisi

Sometimes, it takes stepping back from your life to see where you have come from. For me, I took a step forward into the unknown to see what I was made of. Reflecting can create an experience of pleasure, sadness, or regret, but it will always add to the kaleidoscope of color that makes you who you are. I chose to look at my life through a kaleidoscope because agonizing over the past doesn't bring me happiness. It was in finding that colorful view of my full self, both past and present, that I realized there were times of pain and adversity buried in my life of gratitude. And, perhaps, that is the very thing that gave me such a giving spirit.

I grew up as an only child to parents of Guyanese descent. My incredible parents were the first people to show me the true meaning of giving, as they always gave from the heart and without fanfare. They were generous and kind to everyone around them without ever expecting anything in return. They often gave quietly behind the scenes and I adopted that same quiet approach to charity. My childhood was disciplined, but full of happy memories and surrounded by a large extended family. I can honestly say that I grew up never wanting for anything and because of this I got good grades in school, had many friends, and enjoyed typical teenage experiences.

In my senior year of high school, I met the love of my life while working at a part-time job. Our love story began as friends that quickly turned into best friends, but we could no longer deny the attraction we felt for each other and fell in love. We were dreamers and adventurers. We started a business together before we got married. We had no idea what we were doing, but we tried our hardest to make it work but ended up closing the business just before our first son was born. Our second son was born twenty months later.

My life and dreams became blurred over the next few years as a new mom of two active toddlers. My husband's career was taking off; he seized a promotion opportunity that had us moving from Toronto, Canada to Portland Oregon, USA. It was a complete whirlwind. We packed our bags, our home, and two little babies to move far away from our family and friends. My support network was gone and I felt overwhelmed.

I remember little of our time in Portland Oregon. I was busy taking care of our two boys, setting up a new home in a city I knew nothing about, and figuring out how to navigate our new life. Like all new mothers, I had little time for myself. It was as though I had blinders on to the rest of the world and they would remain on for many years, until our children had grown.

Two years later, some ease returned to our lives when my husband was stationed back in Toronto, near family. However, it wasn't long before a new career opportunity for my husband whisked us off to Chile; this time we had a newborn baby girl and two boys under the age of five. During that chaotic time, I wore my survival mindset like armor. I wore it so well, in fact, that I didn't realize I had it on until twenty-five years later when I was able to focus on myself.

When I reflect on this time of my life, I have no regrets about the choices I made. I chose the path of motherhood and did it with joy and intention. I fully embraced everything that it meant to be a full-time caregiver, I volunteered at my children's schools, became manager of their hockey teams, drove them to all their extracurricular activities, and hosted countless celebrations and events. We certainly had a wonderful social life. My husband and I had a wide circle of friends. Life was full, and I felt blessed . . . but something was missing. It wasn't until most recently that I realized I never took the time to prioritize myself.

The year 2020 was a significant milestone in my life. I turned fifty and I was happy, more than happy, as a wife and a mother. I have lived a blessed life. But, something shifted in me when I turned fifty; I felt as though I needed something more. I started on a journey of discovering what "it" was by focusing on my physical health and exercising hard! Maybe it was the isolation of a pandemic and the negative news streaming over the media. I just knew I needed to step into a different mental and physical challenge. I had no idea what the world had waiting for me, but I felt the pull and I needed to explore it.

I joined an online fitness community to step up my personal fitness and nutrition. I was already active and worked out regularly, but turning half a century was the push I needed to dedicate more time to myself and to get into top physical form. I had always enjoyed going to the gym to work out in group settings because I loved the company and support. But with the Covid lockdowns, this became impossible. Needing to set a goal for myself for this milestone birthday, I chose the online fitness program with a group called Team Strong Girls. The women in my group inspired me and taught me how to prioritize myself, something that I lacked in my adult life. I was given a food plan that had me eating more food than ever before. I meal-prepped for myself and fed my body with healthy and nutritious food that gave me a lot of energy and strength. I planned my workouts as non-negotiable appointments. It was there, for the first time, I fell in love with my workouts and how that made me feel. The online group encouraged vulnerability and supported me every step in my journey; I never felt alone. This community of incredible women cheered me on and was my rock. To celebrate my fitness journey, several of The Strong Girls and I had a photo shoot with a professional photographer.

In front of that camera lens, I felt an energy like I had never before. It wasn't vanity, ego, or even bravado. It was about strength beyond the physical. I would have previously considered having my work out pictures taken professionally a silly endeavor and I was still super uncomfortable in front of the camera. But, by doing it anyway, I cracked open the door to discovering who I truly am, by stepping into this very uncomfortable situation and making myself vulnerable. The photo shoot was the first uncomfortable, yet rewarding experience I've had in a very long time, and this book was another. I'm not a model and I'm not a writer, but by saying yes to new experiences and trying on these new and uncommon opportunities, I have uncovered a part of me I was afraid to own.

I haven't turned into a fitness guru or a supermodel. What I did was focus more on saying "yes" to things that I thought were interesting and brought me happiness. Women often get fully absorbed in motherhood and feel empty when their children have grown because they lose themselves in the process. That wasn't quite my story because I didn't feel lost or unhappy, but I began realizing that fulfillment and purpose were the missing pieces in my life. I didn't wish for more because I didn't know I needed or wanted more. Similarly to the realization someone might have the first time they see the ocean or taste an entirely different cuisine, I discovered there was a whole world I didn't know existed. Being a part of this activity showcasing women to inspire other women was sheer joy.

Historically, women have always supported each other, but it's that taboo word—*selfishness*— that prevents us from focusing on ourselves and discovering what makes us feel strong and empowered. That photo shoot was a day all about me and a chance for me to celebrate myself. But it was also about more than just that. I'm very community-minded. I discovered a new type of community through the women in my fitness challenge. It was one I wanted to see grow.

The Strong Girls fitness group and that photo shoot prompted me to think about what I could do to contribute more to this community. I had been involved with the Make A Wish Foundation for many years. My passion for giving and community inspired the idea of bringing my two worlds together. It was a perfect match. I helped to create a "Giveback Team" with the Strong Girls, which is a ten-week challenge that promotes fitness while raising funds to help children with critical illnesses. To date, we have raised over $35,000, which equates to granting three wishes to kids in need. I have done a lot of fundraising with Make A Wish, but this brought out new feelings and a sense of new purpose. I continued to look for ways to expand my sense of empowerment and joy.

My volunteering with Make A Wish reminded me of another time in my family's life that shook us to the core. My husband was diagnosed with cancer in 2010. It was a total shock and put us through a year we will never forget. My husband and I have always had a symbiotic relationship. He acknowledged that his career successes would never have happened without my support and he was supportive of all my desires and endeavors. My husband traveled a lot, and when the kids started doing extra-curricular activities, my life became one fire drill after another. And I, too, appreciated all the sacrifices he made for us. There was always a reciprocal balance of respect and love. He is the reason for my attitude of gratitude.

Suddenly, that anchor in our family's lives became untethered. We are so grateful that he was able to receive quality treatment at Sunnybrook Hospital in Toronto and recovered quickly. In appreciation, my daughter, Victoria, made bracelets to raise money for the Odette Cancer Center at Sunnybrook Hospital. She was the young age of ten. Victoria sold them to family and friends. I'd attended many hockey banquet fundraisers, and that made me think we could aim bigger with our hospital fundraiser. I rented a banquet hall to have a fundraising Gala. We invited all our family and friends. In five years, we raised over $100,000 for the Sunnybrook Odette Cancer Centre. Fast forward ten years, I continue to flex the charity muscle that had always been there.

From those fundraising efforts, and from seeing the plight of others in circumstances much more dire than our own, I became involved with the Make A Wish Foundation. So many families watch their children, whom they are supposed to protect and nurture, relinquish their childhood to life-threatening disease. I raised money in order to bring hope and a little joy into the lives of these children and their families. The thought of granting wishes made my heart a little lighter, brighter, and my purpose became a lot clearer.

Now I have shed that survival mindset and am ready to embrace all that life offers. The journey from happy to fulfilled and purpose filled was taking shape. From that photo shoot and my charitable journey, the Instagram page *Inspire Always* was born. The founder of Team Strong Girls lived out her "aspire to inspire" motto in her work. I wanted to latch onto that and let other women feel what I felt. I aim to recognize women for who they are and not what they do. I value not only big accomplishments, but also their life as it is. I had learned that when women truly supported each other, incredible things can happen. We need to read more good news in the world and this is what I wanted to do with the Inspire Always page. I wanted to celebrate these fabulous women so that we can all lift each other up by spreading kindness and positivity.

I love a good quote, and I wanted the process of submitting information to be easy. So, the idea behind this project is that each participant shares their favorite quote. They then tell their story. Some are happy, some are funny, some are sad, some are triumphant, and some are truly heartbreaking. I've learned we all have stories to share and in our vulnerability, there is true strength. When we read other peoples' stories, we can often relate and feel like we are not alone, and that is the true strength of community.

My purpose became amazingly clear. I want to give women a platform to share their voice and spread joy. I realized my vision combined charity with the sharing of inspiring stories by women. This collision of giving and community was what I had been looking for my entire life. My "spread kindness" t-shirt campaign was the first of such efforts. I partnered with Million Dollar Smiles to grant a wish for a three-year-old in need of a stem cell donor. Not only was that campaign a huge success, I felt a sense of fulfillment like never before.

You hear that it never feels like work if you can blend your passion with your talent. It took fifty long years to discover that my passion is giving. By taking the time to give to myself, I am able to share my gift of giving to others. Since the start of this project, so many people have told me that this could turn into something big. I struggled with this because I wasn't sure what that would look like. I know now that what I want to do is to build an awesome community whose purpose is to give back to some charities my inspired contributors have created or that they support. I want to celebrate them and connect them to others who share their values. This will be the showcase for all things that give me meaning: community, connection, celebration, compassion, and charity.

"We make a living by what we get, but we make a life by what we give." -Winston Churchill

My journey from happy to being fulfilled was all about discovering my purpose. Unleashing my gift of giving through an inspiring community of women unlocked this purpose that had always been deep inside me. I will continue to say "yes" to all things that inspire my passion for giving. My road through doing the uncomfortable, celebrating myself, making the act of giving my routine, and building a community to spread kindness is how this story ends . . . and an entirely new one begins!

Chapter 19
We Are the Light We Seek in the World

Shruti Singh

"Give a woman a garden and yoga and she will save the world."

Shruti's most defining role is as a mom to two creative and compassionate young women. She feels so much gratitude for being their mom and feels so lucky and blessed.

Shruti is a licensed optician, a yoga and meditation teacher, and a breathwork coach. She is also passionate about reading and gardening. A sizable portion of her bed is occupied by her beloved pooch, Ebony. Any given day, you will find her cooking as a meditative practice, lost in a book, or tinkering in the house. If she had a chance to live as a fictional character, she would definitely be Ms. Marple or Sherlock Holmes because she loves a good murder mystery!

ig: shruti275 ~ fb: shruti.singh
Goodreads: Shruti Singh

Namaste! In Sanskrit, this word means the light in me honors the light in you. I have said this greeting all my life before I even knew its true meaning. I resisted acknowledging this light, energy, or prana, as it is called in India, the land of my birth. Ironically, I studied ophthalmic technology and the physics of light and optics. I tried to downplay the spiritual attributes of this universal energy, but now I realize that no matter how much we resist, life has a way of bringing us to a point where we can't avoid the truth any longer.

I reached that point where layer upon layer of grief and hurt was overwhelming. In a span of a year and half, I lost my younger brother to cancer and then I faced the sudden demise of my marriage after a shocking betrayal. I was broken and traumatized and I desperately wanted to heal, not only for myself, but for both of my daughters, who were just on the cusp of adulthood. I wanted to pull myself together and overcome grief. I was fortunate enough to be exposed to yoga as an eight-year-old, but as the years progressed, my practice had dwindled. I was resistant to meditation, and I realized my focus and attention span were all over the place.

It was entirely serendipitous that, when I joined a conscious entrepreneur course, the teacher led us through a chakra meditation during one session. That led me to a complete paradigm shift. I felt the energy of the light arise out of me, and the spectrum of light kept expanding beyond me. It surpassed my body, the bedroom, the neighborhood, cities, continents, with bursts of light connecting everything in the universe. It was as if everything was comforting me and I no longer felt alone or scared. The green light of the heart chakra grew within me and felt like a fusion of roots and branches. There was no beginning or end—just shoots of green light that enveloped everything.

I finally understood the quote by the Persian poet Rumi, "The wound is the place where the Light enters you." I think it was the wound that let me see the light within. I jumped up and down at that moment, but none of the other participants had a similar experience. I wanted to shout out from the rooftops! It was like a natural adrenaline rush and it was triggered by looking inward. I felt so blessed, knowing that, however insignificant I thought my existence was, life itself is precious. And most vitally, I had turned a page to start a new chapter. I found the inner light was my authentic self, the part of me I had silenced.

Getting back to the practice of yoga and meditation saved me. It helped to uncover the light hidden in me, the one I had forgotten over the decades while I was busy as a mom to two amazing kids. It was exhausting, though, raising kids, one of whom had special needs, moving to a new country, navigating my health issues, and dealing with a difficult marriage. But it wasn't always overwhelming. I remember my teens and early twenties, when I felt a light within me. There were many times when patients for eye examinations asked specifically to be examined by me; they would tell me I had a healing touch. Always the skeptic, I would brush it off. But upon reflection, I realized this magical touch was my inner light, which burned brightly and gave comfort and reassurance to people. Over the years, I lost this gift, or perhaps I covered it up.

I lost my identity when I got married. I had to change my first name because, in India at the time, it was difficult to have an inter-religious marriage. Registering a Hindu-Muslim marriage was fraught with obstacles, including the clerk's refusal to even entertain the idea of pre-registering our marriage. At the time, the only solution appeared to be a name change, and they assured me it was just a perfunctory process. Little did I know I was signing away my identity. Growing up in a secular family, I wasn't strictly religious, so I didn't think twice about this change, which would expedite my marriage. I was so ecstatic at the time that I did not think through what I was doing and how it would impact me. My authentic self, the part of me that made me shine, I let this self down.

Gradually, I lost my sense of self. I was encouraged to hide my pre-marriage name because "people would judge me." In my eagerness to fit in, I covered up the real me and lived a self-effacing existence. I lost my voice and my light, almost to the point of being extinguished.

I held onto my marriage for twenty-three years. As a South Asian woman, it was drilled into me that I had to keep holding on "for the sake of the family" and "for the kids." I kept compromising, hoping for a change in my husband's behavior, but that never happened. In the ensuing years, I lost my self-respect and I think I also lost the respect of my then-husband. I was damaged beyond repair, or so I thought. This moment in my life brings to mind the fable of the Golden Buddha statue in Thailand. Centuries ago, fearing an attack on the temple, the monks covered the gold statue of the Buddha with clay to protect it. I felt like my light was similarly hidden under layers of dirt. I had become a young adult who didn't trust her own intuition, silenced her voice to fit in, and gave up her agency. I disconnected from my purpose in life and fed my own limiting self-beliefs. I didn't realize I was just *existing* without living my purpose. As I focused on my healing, I realized what happened cannot be made right. Some things cannot be fixed. I couldn't get through grief quickly. A sudden death and a life-altering event changed my life. No one is immune to trauma because it is stored deep within our emotional body. As I delved deeper into my own behaviors and responses, it became clear to me that I had been unconsciously programmed by my childhood traumas. I was stuck on a roller coaster of excruciating self-doubt, fear, stress, and anxiety, and this led to a sense of codependency. My innocently ignorant ancestors, with maladaptive parenting and traumas of their own, had passed on this legacy. We are alone, but we are never alone. Just as we carry generational trauma, we also carry generational collective consciousness. I resolved that by trying to heal myself, I would be able to heal my ancestors and, in some way, change the trajectory of the trauma I had inadvertently passed on to my children.

We are the load-bearers of humanity, but we are also living beings amongst the countless life forms that have gone before us, and the countless more that will come after us. I may never heal completely, and I will carry this grief with me always, and that is okay, as long as I am honest and willing to learn, unlearn, and relearn. In every crisis there is a transition, an opportunity for freedom and to accept our whole, imperfect self and give up the need for perfection, our box-up definition of what our lives should be. I no longer feel a need to prove myself; I let go of the fear of uncertainty I carried within. I dropped my ancestral burdens. It doesn't mean that I have become immune to the trauma that is stored deep within my body because every time I am triggered, it unleashes as though from muscle memory. I see it, observe it, sometimes sit with it in acknowledgment, and then I find it doesn't feel as devastating and destructive. I welcome this opportunity to reclaim the person I never got to be because of my self-limiting doubts. But it doesn't mean I can erase and rewrite the past. None of us can do that. I claim the person I see in the mirror, the one with fine wrinkles and gray hair. I look upon her with compassion and love and celebrate as she collects herself with love, without resentment, or guilt, or shame. I see the light radiating out of her as she is now, and that is her authentic self. It doesn't mean there isn't suffering anymore, that she/I don't suffer anymore. As long as there's life, we will have suffering, since, as the Buddha said, "Life is Suffering."

Only when we have hardships can we truly appreciate our blessings. It is only in the darkness that we can see the light. I know now that we each have the capacity to carry our burdens. We only get what we can handle, right? This has been my mantra, an affirmation to help cope with any difficulties in life. Even when my daughter was diagnosed with autism, my first thought was that she chose me because I will help her thrive. Why should this diagnosis lead to anything but joy and celebration in our lives?

This epiphany helped me to delve deeper into meditation philosophies. I understood meditation's true purpose, which was not religious, but instead, it was about letting go of external trappings and the urge we all carry for security. Meditation helped me focus on the present moment and not be overcome by the past or fearful of the future. I knew I had an authentic inner light that had always been there and always will be there.

My recent foray into yoga helped me tap into this collective consciousness, which gives meaning and purpose to our existence. We are part of this energy/light and we are always part of a greater existence. We are alone, but we are never alone. The vibration of this energy is in all of us and we are meant to shine.

By focusing on my inner light, I see the world through the lens of love. I see the world in all its colors . . . the pain and suffering, the joys and sorrows, the love and light through the ages.

In Sanskrit, the word samadhi means, "a state of profound and utterly absorptive contemplation of the Absolute that is undisturbed by desire, anger, or any other ego-generated thought or emotion." The full weight of this idea is becoming apparent to me, as it is what being mindful means. I am alone, yet I am with everyone. The joy of being alive at this moment means embracing the past, which is what brought us to this juncture. If I hadn't made this journey, I wouldn't be here. I just felt I had to leap into this new reality of my life. If I have any hope of surviving, I have to honor my authentic light.

I have felt a longing to teach gardening for mindfulness to individuals with disabilities. I have enjoyed teaching my own children to love the interconnectedness of nature, and to appreciate the life force that seeps through all living beings. Gardening is a deeply meditative and therapeutic practice. Years ago, I read the words of poet and essayist Joseph Addison: "A garden was the habitation of our first parents before the Fall. It is naturally apt to fill the mind with calmness and tranquility, and to lay all its turbulent passions at rest. It gives us a great insight into the contrivance and wisdom of Providence, and suggests innumerable subjects for Meditation."[1] I have been a gardener for several decades precisely for this reason. And though I can't claim to have a green thumb, I am persistent. The cyclical nature of our Canadian seasons aptly mimics our life stages. From the promise of youthful Spring, to the flourish of adult Summers, to the casting off of our cares in Autumn and ultimately the senectitude of our Winters. So much like the mandalas, or "circle" in Sanskrit, which represent the impermanence of human life and are used for meditation practices in Asian and Indigenous North American traditions.

I have pondered in astonishment that our ancestors, over millions of years of evolution, knew the healing powers of nature and tending to nature. This pursuit gives us a sense of connection to our body and our inner being, and a connection to the mystery of life. There is so much wisdom in our collective consciousness.

My health limitations don't permit my body to do the yoga poses, or asanas, I was able to do in my early years of practice. But delving into the true meaning of yoga has allowed me to see how yoga is highly accessible—it's made for all body types and encourages each practitioner to focus on listening to and honoring the body they *have,* not the one they might see on social media. By listening to this inner authentic light, I was able to find my true calling as an accessible yoga and meditation teacher. It took me decades to come to this point; I didn't realize I was preparing for this my whole life. My love for gardening, the early years of yoga training, along with my determined efforts to understand and practice meditation and mindfulness have all led to this moment. It is as if I was climbing a tall mountain in fits and starts, with its many perils, slippery slopes, sharp bends, difficult terrain, and crevasses, and me with no skills whatsoever. And with each step, I learned to understand the ground beneath my feet. I have finally reached a precipice at the peak. I can't go back, I have to go forward by jumping. Leaping from this precipice, I don't know what awaits, but I know I have to jump. There is no safety net, but there is an adrenaline rush, because I am being true and authentic to myself. This is my calling to serve. My dharma, the inherent nature of reality, and this moment is joy and peace.

Chapter 20
Feed Your Soul

Tammy Hudgin

"Be a leader in your life by making choices for you, for what lights you up, for what fuels your passion, for what feeds your soul. Life is meant to be lived and you have the ultimate control over how to live it."

Executive, Mom, Entrepreneur, Professor, Coauthor, Speaker, Bus Driver, House Cleaner, Direct Salesperson, Office Manager. You name it, Tammy has pretty much done it all.

Tammy's wonderful journey through life has taught her many skills and led her to where she is today, a successful Facebook chick and proud mother of two amazing young adults who lives in a mountain village resort.

Life has not always been rosy for Tammy; there have been many ups and downs, but she has learned from all of it, and has discovered some wonderful new things about herself.

Tammy is currently living in Panorama, BC, hiding in the mountains, seeing it through her passion for photography and continuing to build her successful business on social media. She looks forward to all that is still ahead of her—all the new adventures, new ideas, the successes, the failures, the discoveries, the self-love, the beginning of so many amazing opportunities.

We all deserve to live the life we choose to live. Embrace every moment.

www.tammyhudgin.com

fb: tammyhudgincreating

re you a follower? I believe we all are, at some point in our lives. Think about this for a moment . . .

From the day we are born, we are guided down a path full of expectations that are based on what society has implemented. We go to school, then College/University, get a good job, get married, have children, and, if we are lucky, we get to live our passion.

Followers . . .

That's what we have become.

If we never break out of this routine, then will we ever find what truly makes us happy?

Are we willing to break the mold?

Are we willing to do what our hearts truly desire?

When we stop being followers, we will have consequences to deal with. People will make judgments, people will distance themselves, people will see you in a light that doesn't meet their expectations. And, I believe, that is why most of us stay followers.

I have gone through many different cycles in my life, learning about myself, trying new things, establishing businesses, discovering new passions, changing direction for whatever reasons presented themselves. Throughout each of these cycles, I was a follower, but I also broke free in some cases, which ultimately created different paths for me to explore. Oh, and by the way, I am no longer a follower. I made a very unexpected decision for myself.

Was I choosing the right path? Who the hell knows!

What I do know is that I don't regret any of it. How can I?

It is what made me the person I am today and led me here.

When I look back through my life, there are so many things I would change if I could. Some things I am ashamed of, to be honest, but at the time, I never thought about the consequences, or the long-term effects my choices would have. I also made some significant decisions that guided me down paths I didn't expect at all. If you were to ask me, back in my teens, where I was going to be at this age,

I would never in a million years have said here. At age fifty-three, I'm living in Panorama, BC, 4000 feet up the mountain, enjoying photography as a hobby, running my own business that allows me to work from anywhere, and I have two amazing children.

Why would this have been unthinkable for me at that time? Because I didn't know any of this existed. I stayed within my parameters of living in Ontario, building a business, being a Mom. I couldn't imagine not living near my children, not being part of their lives as they built their own futures.

I didn't know what was possible because I was a follower. What would happen if I went in a direction that the rest of society was going to judge me for? What would my children think? Would they support my decisions?

I didn't realize the effect that my role as a follower was having until I saw how my behavior influenced my daughter's life. You always think your kids will be okay; you always think that you are doing the best you can for them. But, sometimes, we don't see what is right in front of our noses. I regret not being the Mom I should have been when my daughter battled mental health issues, because I couldn't understand or relate to how she was feeling. Mental health is not something that anyone should have to battle and, as parents, I think we need to be more aware of the signs and of how we can help. The best news I can give you is that we came together and I am happy to say that my daughter is on a great path to a whole new life. I couldn't be more proud of how far she has come.

I believe that each cycle I have traveled through allowed me to look at myself over and over again. It allowed me to see who I was becoming and decide if that was the person I wanted to be. It gave me the chance to change myself, to release negative energy and bring in new energy. It gave me the power to make new decisions and say *yes* to trying new things. (Never be afraid to try. The worst thing that could happen is you'll find out you don't like it.)

I learned that I needed to look at myself, *really* look at who I was and what I was becoming. I was sharing a home with my ex-husband and basically lived either in my bedroom or my office. I spent time with my boyfriend, Doug, in his basement apartment. My son had purchased a home with his girlfriend and was starting a new life, and my daughter was reaching a turning point in her life and figuring out what her next steps would be. So, where did that leave me? What life was I living? Doug and I had just gotten back together, and we needed to decide about our future. It was time for me to figure out what I wanted and who I was.

It can be hard to look at yourself in the mirror and admit the "negative" points about yourself, but we need to do it in order to see the opposite side of the spectrum, don't we? *Yes*, positive words are *key*, and understanding the power of our words and thoughts is important. But at the same time, we can never be better versions of ourselves if we don't look at and embrace the icky parts. We need to accept whatever mistakes we have made, accept our faults, and move forward to improve them. It is important to look at and focus on what we want. Trust me, it really is a cool experience when you face yourself and then set goals to change for the better, I promise! I still have more work to do, but I love knowing that I have more cycles to come, and that I'm getting better at being *me*!

So, let's jump to how I got to where I am today.

I was born in Nova Scotia, lived in Ontario from the age of three, and at the ripe old age of fifty-three, decided to pack up and move to Panorama, BC, a mountain resort village in the Purcell Mountain Range. I was living in British Columbia within two years of making a decision to do so.

A decision that would affect every single person in my life.

A decision that meant leaving my children behind in Ontario.

A decision to walk away from my family.

A decision to walk away from my friends.

A decision to move away with my boyfriend, whom I had been previously separated from for six months.

A decision to start all over.

A decision to no longer be a follower.

Was it hard? Damn right!

Do I regret it? Not at all!

My life has had ups and downs, just like everyone else, and somehow I figured out how to manage it all.

I married, had two amazing kids, separated from my husband, then shared a home with my ex-husband for the next thirteen years, worked in the corporate world, quit, did odd jobs here and there (including working as a bus driver where I had so much fun with the kids), started in direct sales, jumped on board the Facebook craze when it launched, way back when, and it all led me to here.

I have my own business, working within the wonderful world of Facebook (no need for details, that's the boring stuff) and have both of my children's support in moving here, (hoping they will join me one day, wink wink), a group of friends, and business friends that I am grateful for, every single day (I wouldn't be here with my business without them), a small but cool condo that has mountain views and a backyard that is a photographer's dream. I get to work at my business and enjoy my passion for photography while exploring the spectacular province of British Columbia!

The best part of getting to where I'm at right now, in this moment of my life, was realizing I was being a follower and making the decision to lead my own life. Every lesson learned, mistake made, dream created, and desire fostered has put me in charge of my own decisions, my own dreams, and, ultimately, my own version of living that is best for me!

Don't follow the leader. Be your own leader and live out all the dreams you can imagine!

For me, I see visions of women's retreats, places where I can share my knowledge and show others how to feed their soul, to discover themselves, to meet other women who carry the same thoughts/ideas/passions, to have a few days of just being themselves.

Can you imagine having that?

When was the last time you gave yourself that gift?

When was the last time you decided that today was going to be all about you?

The biggest thing I've learned in my life is that you have to treat yourself, feed your soul, and find that special energy that makes you feel alive. The daily routines of life, of society, of the people we surround ourselves with, can catch up to us if we don't take the time to do self-care, self-love (or, as my girlfriend, Suzanne Forster calls it, "soul-care") . . . Feed Your Soul!

You know what is crazy about that last statement I made? I didn't learn this until I was in my fifties. I never thought about it, I guess. I mean, sure, I did the manicures, the pedicures, the dinners out with girlfriends, the usual things we do to make ourselves feel better. What I never really understood was that I could feed my soul just by going for a walk—the power of a walk! Taking two hours out of my day, and going, disappearing, putting my phone on mute, and walking (of course, I do love bringing my camera). That walk allows me to clear my mind, to focus on my current surroundings, to hear the birds, the swish of the leaves, the colors, the smells, and it always puts a smile on my face.

It allows me to escape for a little while.

To rejuvenate, to feed my soul.

When I am on these walks, I sometimes run into other people, and on one particular day, their reactions struck me when I would say, "Good Morning" as I passed. Some respond smiling, others seem more grumpy, but what this made me realize is that the majority of people are afraid of life. The fear of letting people in, the fear of smiling, the fear of having contact, the fear of . . . we live in a world of fear.

As long as we are afraid of life, we will never uncover our light. We can't, it's just not possible.

Because if we never say yes, if we never jump, if we never try new things, if we never make a change, we can never find that light. We will continue to be a follower, listening to what society says, obeying the rules "they" put into place for us. Until you make the decision to be *you*, to find yourself, to find what you love, what you desire, you can't uncover your light because you will never connect with what feeds your soul.

Now, on the flip side of things, you can meet some amazing people throughout your journey who will support you, cheer you on, encourage you, inspire and motivate you. These people . . . *keep them around!* Trust me, there will be days when you need someone to help you make a move or change your mindset to move forward. These are the people who you can share your ideas, your passions, your words. These are the people who become your inner circle, the ones you hug tight. They will be your cheerleaders, and we all deserve to have cheerleaders! We all are powerful in our own way. As soon as we find what feeds our souls, what brings us to life, what fires us up, and leads us to uncover that light that we have been searching for!

Make no mistake, this won't be easy. You will go through a variety of emotions as you take your next steps towards your light. You need to embrace these emotions, understand them and how they are affecting you. When you start to notice that there is more happiness inside your soul, then you will know that you have made the right decisions.

I still hold emotion around the idea of not being present as my children build their lives, but the reality is that I am only a plane ride away. I can still be a part of their lives and I have a place where my future grandchildren can come and experience life at a different level. The best of both worlds, two loving homes that will provide them with many opportunities to live their passions and be leaders in their own lives.

As you are walking towards finding what feeds your soul, I want you to be very aware of all the different signs that will appear. Understand the signs and the significance of them. Understand at what point they first showed themselves and you will start to realize that you have been manifesting this right from the beginning. I have been working through this myself and am quite amazed at how many times things were presented over my lifetime that ultimately led me to this village. Without even knowing, I have been envisioning this since I first visited British Columbia back in my early twenties. At that time, I was escaping something in my life in Ontario, and I dwelled on what I was fleeing from, instead of seeing any importance in what BC meant to me, or why I had chosen this place as my haven. I never thought much of BC back then, or the idea of wanting to live here.

BC came back into my life when I was at an impasse, was in limbo, and wondered what the future held. The province gave me the opportunity to explore my photography more with spectacular backdrops and allowed me to get out in nature to feed my soul. It has presented me with the chance to build a new business, to share my love of this area, to help others to feed their souls too!

I feel alive again!

I have a purpose again!

I have something that ignites me inside!

A new beginning that will lead to opening and shutting many doors, but ultimately, will feed my soul!

We all have choices, and we need to either accept or change the choices we make. You can choose to be a follower, or you can break free and start finding yourself again. Either way, it is your choice! There will be consequences and you need to be okay with accepting them, but if you never take that first step, how will you ever find out?

The world just spent two years in limbo; we were given time to really reflect on our lives and how we were living them. So, let me ask you . . . what steps are you taking next to feed your soul, to uncover your light?

Chapter 21
Becoming the Light

Lisa Pinnock

"True transformation happens amidst darkness and doubt, but uncovering the brilliance that awaits on the other side is so worth the effort. The world needs your light to shine brightly."

Lisa is an educator, musician, multipreneur, and lifelong learner. She is a bestselling co-author of *Women Let's Rise*, an award-winning publication by Golden Brick Road Publishing House.

She loves inspiring women to step into their power and light through community building, advocacy work, and healthy eating with Epicure. Lisa leads a local group of heart-centered entrepreneurial women with FemCity, where she is a Global Member and facilitates workshops on their platform. She is excited about a new venture as a Certified Circle Leader with WomanSpeak, a global organization devoted to unleashing the brilliance of women's voices through unique public speaking practices.

Lisa's involvement as a founding member of Diversity, Equity, and Inclusion Committees with Epicure and FemCity has fueled her mission to highlight and amplify the voices of diverse, marginalized communities. She firmly believes that representation matters, and that our society is strongest when we embrace the full spectrum of humanity.

Lisa brings decades of combined experience and leadership in a myriad of fields, including music education and performance, classroom teaching, liturgical planning, mentorship, and most recently, lead authoring two book projects with GBR. She is honored to collaborate with the incredible women who have poured their hearts into writing Volumes One and Two of *Uncover Your Light: Empowering Stories of Hope and Resilience*.

ig: lisampinnock ~ fb: lisamariepinnock

li: lisapinnock ~ Goodreads: Lisa Pinnock

Traversing the Dark Spaces

"The journey of the dark night of the soul is where we learn who we are, without people telling us."
- The Requiem of the Moon Poetry

I don't know exactly when I slipped on the floor. But, there I lay, sobbing in a crumpled heap. The guttural sounds emanating from my belly seemed other-worldly . . . could a human actually make such noises? Yeah, it's possible. I've come to realize that heartache and unresolved pain can bring up things you'd rather keep under wraps. But hiding them away serves no one.

And so the body-heaving sobs continued for a while, taking on a rhythm all their own, with no predictable end in sight. I eventually had to change position when one area of the blanket covering me became soaked with tears. And that's when I looked up and noticed the room was completely dark. How fitting, I thought. I welcomed the dark in that moment. It was easier to withhold all of this from the light of day. That way, I wouldn't feel compelled to explain these overwhelming feelings of despair and sadness. They could just remain our little secret, between me and the darkness. No one would ever need to know.

What happened next came as an unexpected but necessary jolt to the system. I pulled off the saturated covers, sat up straight, and with a voice I hardly recognized, I yelled into the pitch black room, "So . . . whaddya gonna do? Just sit here? Are you gonna stay in the dark, or find your light?" That voice was my own, but it was surfacing in such a strident, authoritative manner that I was taken aback. It was almost as if my higher self had arrived on the scene and proceeded to give me a good shake while pointing out the obvious—enough was enough. I had taken time to grieve, to let my inner child have a full-blown tantrum all over the living room floor. And now, present-day Lisa had a choice to make: stay in the shadows of self-doubt and ego-driven confusion, or move into a state of self-love, purpose, and *light*.

I'm grateful for making the latter choice that night, and it came with immediate rewards. By choosing to pick myself up from the floor, literally and figuratively, I sent a message to my overwrought system: It was safe . . . *I* was safe, and the high-alert mode I was existing in could finally loosen its grip. I began to notice things around me with fresh eyes, as though a thin veil had been lifted to expose the tiniest sliver of hope and inner peace. At this juncture of utter despair, I saw the value of leaning into a reservoir of strength and trusting my intuition to guide me home . . . back to myself. The message was received loud and clear, with such veracity that it couldn't be ignored: Lisa had stuff to do, and she wasn't going to get any of it done by staying in that dark place. It was time to *rise* and *shine*.

It Only Takes a Spark

One of the guiding tenets of this compilation was a question I asked myself repeatedly: "How do we shine our light brightly when we've lost touch with who we are?" From the moment I envisioned the book you're reading right now, I felt this point of inquiry deserved exploration, and that looking within would be the only pathway to move us through the darkness.

There are things in our lives—upheaval, loss, pain, disappointment—that come about to crack us open, to lay bare the assumptions we hold about ourselves and others, to bring awareness to the programming and patterns that keep us stuck on a never-ending hamster wheel of our own making. But here's what I've come to learn through some of the darkest moments: They provide opportunities to trust ourselves and the light shining within us, even when that light has been dimmed to a mere flicker. Being a light for others begins with igniting our inner spark. Sounds simple enough, yet it's profoundly challenging when we can't see a clear pathway ahead. For me, it has always come down to an unshakeable knowing of God's love and being created with a light that cannot be extinguished. That belief serves as a foundation for my life's purpose, keeping me grounded in my oneness with an unending source of abundance and goodness. Throughout the COVID-19 pandemic, I've had the privilege of singing each week at my parish's live-streamed mass. Having this outlet to offer my voice in worship and praise, and to seek God's comfort and grace during challenging times, has been nothing short of miraculous. If you've known me for more than five minutes, you'll understand that music is my life force—always has been, and continues to be, my sanctuary. One particular song, "Oceans" by Hillsong Worship, struck a chord deep within me from the first time I heard it:

"You call me out upon the waters, the great unknown where feet may fail.

And there I find You in the mystery; in oceans deep, my faith will stand."

These lyrics reminded me that we were never promised smooth waters at all times. When the waves came crashing down, I found strength and solace in my God-given light to bring me safely back to shore.

Here for the Lessons

Commitment to personal growth is not for the faint of heart. Ask any of the incredible women who have shared their self-discovery journeys within this compilation. I'll bet they would say that despite any pain or discomfort, every single step was worth the effort.

As I write these words, my first co-authored book, *Women Let's Rise,* recently celebrated its one-year anniversary. The chapter I contributed to that compilation described how I learned to trust my intuition and what that looked like in my life over the span of many decades. Through this experience, my passion for writing as a means of self-expression was no longer dormant, and I'm forever grateful for the opportunity the book gave me to burst open the floodgates of creativity, self-love, and healing.

The simple phrase, "here for the lessons," has been my mantra the past few years. It serves as a daily reminder of my commitment to growth in body, mind, and soul. By "lessons," I'm not referring to book learning, but rather, the insights gained from experiences that crack you wide open to reveal the truth that lies within. Those can be the toughest kind, yet they are the most valuable by far.

So many transformative lessons have been gleaned over the past three years. It may sound like a relatively short time frame, but *wowzers*, was there ever a lot of growth packed in there! What I share here is not meant to be prescriptive or a recipe for a particular outcome; this isn't a "How to Heal in 90-days" type of formula. Instead, I offer these words as a source of affirmation to the scores of women who are, or have been, on their own paths toward mental, emotional, and spiritual wellness. Granted, what that looks like for each of us will vary greatly, but knowing that others have walked similar roads can provide much-needed solace and give hope when we need it most. There's an inherent beauty in speaking your truth that I find so fascinating: One person's experiences can become another's survival guide.

Loving the Totality of You

"I long, as does every human being, to be at home wherever I find myself." - *Maya Angelou*

I'm pretty sure we can all strongly recall our first loves. It's an exhilarating feeling to put all of our attention, energy, and emotional being into another person. It's breathtaking, all-encompassing, and, well, often heart-breaking too. My first love was a wonderful guy from my university days who I'm grateful to still consider a trusted friend.

But what if we put the same energy and focus on appreciating ourselves? What amazing things could come from the wellspring of attention? These are questions I never really considered in my years as a young wife and mother—in fact, they didn't even appear on my radar. It's only in recent years that I've contemplated the massive benefits of loving myself first, without explanations or apologies. And what a freeing, transformative, grounding process it has been.

I'm not going to lie—my journey toward a place of truly valuing and loving myself hasn't been smooth or linear. I recall one period in particular that was very challenging. Rewind to the summer of 2020, when I found myself in a dark place on many levels. And being amid a global pandemic certainly didn't help. Thankfully, I connected with a wonderful program through The Proctor Gallagher Institute. Anyone who has experienced the teachings of the legendary Bob Proctor will know how life-altering they can be, if you're willing to do the work. I started sifting through the material in *The Self-Image of Your Dreams* portion of the program, and was instantly met with resistance from within. Saying kind, supportive words to myself while looking straight in the mirror was completely foreign and quite uncomfortable. Years upon years of limiting beliefs and false stories were congregating all at once in my head, screaming things like, *You can't be serious! Do you really believe that? How can you even say that with a straight face?* In the early days, I was in tears as I practiced the exercise. But with time, patience, and lots of repetition, it became easier to get through the thirty-five personal affirmations with dry eyes. I even found myself smiling at my reflection in the mirror more and more often. In retrospect, shedding all those tears was a cathartic release of a ton of stored-up emotions. They needed to come to the surface and be acknowledged for me to let them go and step into a place of healing. Slowly but surely, I began to see myself through kind eyes instead of harsh, critical ones. Far too often, we only give ourselves a fraction of the compassion and understanding that we freely offer to others. Once we become aware of the ways we lack self-love, we create the possibility of choosing a different path, one where we can love ourselves without hesitation or reservation.

Over the past few years, and with the help of several amazing mentors (you know who you are), I've learned to incorporate an array of tools to promote a deeper sense of self in my daily life. One favorite activity has been creating mantras to weave into my routines. My dear friend and intuitive coach, Sara McCready of *Illuminated Joy*, suggested saying a mantra while showering. In our sessions, I learned that water has the power to heal and transmute the negative energies we pick up during our day-to-day interactions, bringing us back to a place of alignment. Here is what I wrote and still recite daily:

With this water I wash away all negativity brought today

Whether in thought, or word, or deed—my sovereignty I will not concede

So I stand in my truth and my power to heal, knowing God's plan will be revealed

So I thank Him now for this precious day, and all the blessings that
are coming my way.

Learning to love ourselves is a daily choice. Just like being in a
state of gratitude takes constant work, inhabiting spaces of joy and
abundance is a choice we can make with each new day. Here's what
I know for sure: being loving and compassionate with yourself first
is a skill we can develop over time, with consistent practice. The rewards we'll reap are beyond measure and ours for the taking. So tell
me, Dear Reader, what will your choice be today?

Freedom in Forgiveness

Many of us believe that it's hard to forgive, whether we have
in mind ourselves or others, and that only special people can do it,
like Jesus or Nelson Mandela. But I think the first step is to understand that by offering forgiveness, you're not exonerating the person
who has wronged you. It's more about liberating yourself. It's a gift
of self-love, and your ability to let go is what matters, not the other
person's reaction.

We create space within ourselves by letting go of our past. You
can think of forgiveness as a springboard to a higher state of vibration. Offering forgiveness also sends out a healing energy that comes
back to you. It's like offering a source of healing to yourself. I also
believe that by forgiving, we cut the cord that kept us tethered to
that hurt, so it doesn't show up in other ways, or in future relationships.

You may wonder what these acts of forgiveness could look like
in your life? I recently discovered the concept of "Radical Forgiveness," which is about opening up to the idea that everything in our
lives happens for a reason. Yup, including the messy stuff. That may
be difficult to imagine when there's trauma or suffering involved.
You might think, "How can *that* grief have a purpose?" But amazing
shifts in perspective can happen when we recognize that something
valuable can come from our deepest pain. It's a matter of reframing
our wounds to consider, "What is this situation trying to teach me?"

When I was introduced to the ancient Hawaiian Ho'Oponopo-
no prayer, I was facing a time when my ability to forgive was in deep

decline. What struck me first about this prayer was its simplicity. Just a few lines, repeated as many times as needed, to feel a sense of calm and release. If you're not familiar with these words, they are: "I'm sorry. Please forgive me (I forgive myself). Thank you. I love you." I invite you to try them for yourself.

I approached this prayer in a way similar to my mirror-work. At first, it was hard to be unreserved, and when I was, it was hard to keep my eyes dry. But once I reflected inward through my mind's eye and started reciting the prayer, albeit half-heartedly at first, I felt a shift within my being. *I'm sorry. Please forgive me (I forgive myself). Thank you. I love you.* The heaviness I was carrying seemed to peel away with each repetition. *I'm sorry. Please forgive me (I forgive myself). Thank you. I love you.* My perspective was changing. I understood that life wasn't happening *to* me, but *for* me. *I'm sorry. Please forgive me (I forgive myself). Thank you. I love you.* I shed so many layers of dense emotions that kept me stuck in an endless loop of self-doubt and "not-enoughness." *I'm sorry. Please forgive me (I forgive myself). Thank you. I love you.*

My deepest desire for you, Dear Reader, is that you'll come to a similar place of self-love and forgiveness through the stories within these pages. For me, an incredible dream has already manifested because you are reading these words. My wish is that you'll take away exactly what you need to truly see yourself, and to become the light that's always been inside you.

Acknowledgments

To my incredible mom—a role model who always finds the light. To my amazing children, Emily, Thomas, Ben, and Caroline, who fuel my light. And to my ever-expanding posse of extraordinary true friends, who include my wonderful brothers and my "sisters in-love."

   - Sara Curleigh-Parsons

To my favorite Lantern Bearers: my parents, Lloyd and Mary; my sisters, Elizabeth and Belinda; my children, Theresa and Simon. With love and gratitude,

   - Lesley James

I am beyond grateful for my parents who, from an early age, instilled in me a love and curiosity of nature through family hikes and adventurous travel.

   - Karen Richter

To my wonderful mom and family, amazing husband, Rodney, and beautiful daughters, Zoey, Rylie, and Evynne, thank you for your constant support and encouragement. To my Lord Jesus Christ, I wouldn't be who I am today without You.

   - Ada S. Lau

Thank you to my amazing Mum, family, and friends, especially Des, Jerome, Taylor, and Autumn, for inspiring and encouraging me to be bold and follow my dreams. Thank you GBR for this wonderful opportunity.

   - Caron Bernard

Thank you to my parents, for always doing everything in your power; my siblings for being my anchors; my two sons, Justin and Brandon, I'm honoured to be your Mother and I learn from you both; Bruce, for your neverending support and patience; and to those special few who shared their meaningful thoughts which contributed to sharing my story.

- Louisa Tam

I am so very grateful for my Mahal—hopelessly committed to this crazy adventure we call life—and to each of our children for choosing us to be their bow. I would like to dedicate this chapter to my Moon sister, Kali, whose wisdom inspired me to find healing through writing. And a special thank you to my friend and healer, Maria, who has kept me balanced. Love, Light, and Peace.

- Lesa Ritchie Craig

To all who have crossed my path and for those yet to come, thank you. I am evolving because of you. Love to my family and friends. I am grateful for Lisa's vision and for the support of my co-authors.

- Crystal MacGregor

I dedicate this chapter to all those that are struggling and feel alone out there. Believe in yourself and never give up. To Riley, no matter what the years will bring, I will forever be grateful that you came into my life.

- Janet H. Lau

Thank you to my family, friends, clients, and those who believed in me throughout my journey of building my business. With every person who I assisted or worked with, I've increased my knowledge of Facebook and continue to use it to build a successful business. You all supported and encouraged me to continue on this path and it led me to sharing my knowledge in this book, and for that, I am truly grateful.

- Tammy Hudgin

To the beans, my heart, you are the reason for everything I do. To my family and friends, thank you for holding space for me. To my Creating Space Community, thank you for allowing me into your hearts, your lives, and your homes. This is for you.
      - Julie Clark Wobbe

So blessed for my incredible husband Eric, my amazing children Thomas, Nicholas, and Victoria. To my supportive parents, family, friends, Team Strong Girls, and the *Inspire Always* community. I am grateful for you all.
      - Marcia Agius

I am so grateful to my dear friend Sandra Didomenico for introducing me to this opportunity to share my story. Thank you to Lisa Pinnock and Ky-Lee Hanson for all your help, support, and advice with my chapter.
      - Antonietta Botticelli

From the bottom of my heart, I would like to thank my parents, my in-laws (who are no longer with us), my siblings and their families, and my dearest friends for their shoulders to lean on and cry on, during one of my life's darkest moments. To my amazing family—John, Nathan, and Nicholas: Thank you for your unconditional love and support in everything I do and for giving me the courage to share my story. I love you all so very much!
      - Amy P.K. Wong

To my parents and my dear husband, Enio, thanks for always supporting me. My kids, Vanessa and Dante: You are my inspiration. Thank you to my friend Antonietta Botticelli for embarking on this project with me.
      - Sandra Didomenico

I would like to thank my family, especially Lily and Zion, and friends whose love reminds me every day that I too can love my true self. Thank you,

   - Nicole Bolden

To my friends and family who have supported me through my journey, I couldn't do this without you. To Denise T., thank you for encouraging me to share my story, and to Linda B. for being my accountability buddy.

   - Christa Greenland

Thanks to my husband, David, and our children, Nicole and Kayla, the rest of my family, my friends, including Lisa, and the other coauthors who have inspired and encouraged me on this life-changing adventure.

   - Carol Ward

Thank you to my siblings, Asim, Nazim, and Nazima, and my friend, Ayesha, for all your love and support and always keeping me intellectually curious and grounded.

   - Shruti Singh

Love fills my heart for the two people who make me be a better woman every day: my children, Layla and Jaxon. Shine bright, be brave, and live authentically in who you are.

   - Carole Blackburn

To my family and friends who've supported me in a myriad of ways through the years. To my parents, Kay and Lloyd Pinnock, who are my rocks. To Ky-Lee Hanson, Lola Small, and all the phenomenal women who contributed to this project. Your light and grace inspire me daily.

   - Lisa Pinnock

GOLDEN BRICK ROAD
PUBLISHING HOUSE

Link arms with us as we pave new paths to a better and more expansive world.

Golden Brick Road Publishing House (GBRPH) is an independently initiated boutique press created to provide social-innovation entrepreneurs, experts, and leaders a space in which they can develop their writing skills and content to reach existing audiences as well as new readers.

Serving an ambitious catalogue of books by individual authors, GBRPH also boasts a unique co-author program that capitalizes on the concept of "many hands make light work." GBRPH works with our authors as partners. Thanks to the value, originality, and fresh ideas we provide our readers, GBRPH books are now available in bookstores across North America and have won multiple awards.

We aim to develop content that drives positive social change while empowering and educating our members to help them strengthen themselves and the services they provide to their clients.

Iconoclastic, ambitious, and set to enable social innovation, GBRPH is helping our writers/partners make cultural change one book at a time.

Inquire today at
www.goldenbrickroad.pub